Metabolic Confusion Diet Cookbook for Endomorph Women

28-Day Meal Plan to Unlock the Secrets of Weight Loss and Turbocharge Your Metabolism with Proven, Easy-to-Follow Recipes

Jennifer Napier

SCAN THE QR CODE AND IMMEDIATELY ACCESS YOUR 3 SPECIAL BONUSES IN DIGITAL FORMAT!

🔥 **Bonus 1: Dining Out Without Derailing Your Diet**

🔥 **Bonus 2: Recognizing Your Body Type**

🔥 **Bonus 3: Weekly Grocery Planner**

TABLE OF CONTENTS

Cottage Cheese with Sliced Radishes ... 77

CHAPTER 1

THE SCIENCE OF METABOLIC CONFUSION

Introduction to Metabolic Confusion: Understanding the Basics

Welcome to the world of metabolic confusion, where traditional weight management strategies are reimagined. Instead of fixating on calorie counting and rigid dietary rules, metabolic confusion emphasizes variation and adaptation. By harnessing the body's innate ability to adapt to changes in diet and exercise, this approach promotes sustainable weight loss and optimal metabolic efficiency. At its core, metabolic confusion leverages strategic variations in macronutrient composition, meal timing, and calorie intake to keep the body guessing and prevent metabolic adaptation. The benefits extend beyond weight loss, encompassing improved energy levels, enhanced athletic performance, and overall well-being. With metabolic confusion, you can embark on a journey toward lasting health and vitality, free from the constraints of traditional dieting methods.

The Principles Behind Metabolic Confusion

In today's fast-paced world, the quest for optimal health and vitality is more important than ever. Metabolic confusion offers a refreshing approach, embracing flexibility, variety, and adaptability in nutrition. By constantly varying your dietary intake – from calorie levels to macronutrient ratios and meal timings – metabolic confusion keeps your metabolism guessing and your body on its toes, like conducting a symphony of flavors and nutrients. But it's about much more than just numbers on a scale; it's about nourishing your body, mind, and soul with wholesome, delicious foods that fuel your vitality and zest for life. As you embark on this transformative journey, know that you're part of a vibrant community of like-minded individuals, cheering each other on towards their goals. So, are you ready to embrace the principles of metabolic confusion and unlock your full potential? Let's dive in and embrace this adventure together!

How Metabolic Flexibility Relates to Weight Loss

Metabolic flexibility plays a crucial role in achieving and maintaining weight loss goals by enabling the body to efficiently switch between different fuel sources and adapt to changing metabolic demands. When individuals have good metabolic flexibility, their bodies can effectively utilize carbohydrates, fats, and even ketones for energy, depending on availability and need. This metabolic adaptability is essential for optimizing fat metabolism, regulating blood sugar levels, and supporting overall metabolic health.

In the context of weight loss, metabolic flexibility allows individuals to better respond to dietary changes and fluctuations in calorie intake. For example, during periods of calorie restriction, metabolic flexibility enables the body to efficiently mobilize stored fat for energy, facilitating fat loss while preserving lean muscle mass. Conversely, during periods of increased calorie intake, metabolic flexibility ensures that excess calories are utilized for energy production rather than stored as fat, helping to prevent weight gain.

Metabolic flexibility is closely linked to insulin sensitivity, which is a key factor in regulating blood sugar levels and facilitating glucose uptake into cells for energy. When individuals have good insulin sensitivity, their bodies are better able to effectively metabolize carbohydrates and prevent excessive insulin secretion, which can contribute to fat storage and insulin resistance. By improving insulin sensitivity through dietary strategies such as carbohydrate cycling and intermittent fasting, individuals can enhance their metabolic flexibility and support weight loss efforts.

Overall, metabolic flexibility is essential for achieving sustainable weight loss by allowing the body to efficiently adapt to changes in dietary intake and energy demands. By optimizing metabolic flexibility through dietary and lifestyle interventions, individuals can enhance fat metabolism, regulate blood sugar levels, and improve overall metabolic health, ultimately leading to successful and long-lasting weight loss results.

Biological Mechanisms of Metabolic Confusion

Metabolic confusion operates on the principle of constantly challenging and stimulating the body's metabolic processes to prevent adaptation and optimize efficiency. This concept relies on several biological mechanisms to achieve its goals. One key mechanism is metabolic flexibility, which refers to the ability of cells to switch between different fuel sources, such as carbohydrates, fats, and proteins, based on availability and energy demands. By incorporating variations in macronutrient intake, metabolic confusion enhances metabolic flexibility, enabling the body to efficiently utilize diverse energy sources.

Another crucial mechanism is hormesis, which is the adaptive response of cells and organisms to low doses of stress or stimuli. Metabolic confusion induces hormetic responses through intermittent fasting, calorie cycling, and exercise variations, among other strategies. These mild stressors trigger beneficial adaptations at the cellular level, such as enhanced mitochondrial function, improved insulin sensitivity, and increased fat oxidation.

It's confusion influences hormonal regulation, particularly hormones involved in appetite control, energy expenditure, and fat metabolism. By manipulating factors like meal timing, nutrient composition, and calorie intake, metabolic confusion modulates hormone levels to support weight loss and metabolic health. For example, cycling carbohydrate intake can regulate insulin levels, while intermittent fasting may increase levels of growth hormone and catecholamines, promoting fat burning and preserving lean muscle mass. Metabolic confusion exploits the concept of nutrient partitioning, which refers to the allocation of nutrients for different physiological processes, such as energy production, storage, and maintenance of bodily functions. Through strategic dietary interventions and exercise protocols, metabolic confusion aims to optimize nutrient partitioning to favor fat loss over fat storage and promote muscle preservation.

Metabolic confusion harnesses a range of biological mechanisms to disrupt metabolic homeostasis, promote adaptive responses, and ultimately facilitate sustainable weight loss and metabolic health. By understanding these underlying mechanisms, individuals can tailor their approach to metabolic confusion and maximize its effectiveness in achieving their health and fitness goals.

Metabolism Adaptation: A Biological Perspective

Metabolism adaptation, viewed from a biological perspective, is the body's remarkable ability to adjust and regulate its metabolic processes in response to changes in dietary intake, energy expenditure, and environmental factors. At its core, metabolism adaptation reflects the body's innate drive to maintain homeostasis and ensure survival in the face of fluctuating conditions.

From a biological standpoint, metabolism adaptation involves a complex interplay of physiological mechanisms orchestrated by various hormones, enzymes, and signaling pathways. When individuals undergo changes in their dietary habits or energy balance, the body initiates a series of adaptive responses to maintain energy balance and regulate metabolic functions.

One of the key mechanisms involved in metabolism adaptation is the regulation of metabolic rate, which refers to the rate at which the body burns calories to produce energy. In response to changes in calorie intake, the body adjusts metabolic rate to match energy expenditure, ensuring that energy balance is maintained. This adjustment in metabolic rate occurs primarily through changes in thyroid hormone levels, which play a central role in regulating metabolic rate and energy metabolism.

It involves changes in fuel utilization and nutrient partitioning, whereby the body shifts its preference for different fuel sources based on availability and demand. For example, during periods of calorie restriction, the body may prioritize the use of stored fat for energy to compensate for reduced calorie intake. Conversely, during periods of increased calorie intake, the body may preferentially use carbohydrates for energy, while storing excess calories as fat for future use. Metabolism adaptation encompasses adjustments in appetite regulation, energy expenditure, and metabolic efficiency to maintain energy balance over time. Hormones such as leptin, ghrelin, and insulin play critical roles in signaling hunger and satiety, regulating energy expenditure, and modulating metabolic rate in response to changes in dietary intake and body composition.

Metabolism adaptation is a dynamic and highly orchestrated process that enables the body to adjust and adapt to changes in its environment and energy balance. Understanding the biological mechanisms underlying metabolism adaptation is essential for developing effective strategies for weight management, metabolic health, and overall well-being. By leveraging our understanding of metabolism adaptation, we can optimize dietary and lifestyle interventions to support metabolic flexibility, promote fat loss, and achieve long-term success in achieving health and fitness goals.

The Role of Hormones in Metabolic Responses

Hormones play a pivotal role in orchestrating metabolic responses throughout the body, influencing processes such as energy expenditure, nutrient utilization, and fat storage. Understanding the intricate interplay between hormones and metabolism is essential for optimizing health and achieving fitness goals.

Insulin, produced by the pancreas, is a key hormone involved in regulating blood sugar levels and facilitating the uptake of glucose into cells for energy or storage. Elevated insulin levels, often triggered by consuming high-carbohydrate meals, promote the storage of excess glucose as glycogen in the liver and muscles. However, chronically high insulin levels can lead to insulin resistance, impairing the body's ability to effectively use glucose and increasing the risk of metabolic disorders like type 2 diabetes and obesity.

Another hormone, glucagon, acts in opposition to insulin by promoting the release of stored glucose from the liver to maintain blood sugar levels during fasting or periods of low carbohydrate intake. By stimulating gluconeogenesis (the production of glucose from non-carbohydrate sources), glucagon helps sustain energy levels and prevent hypoglycemia.

Leptin and ghrelin are hormones involved in regulating appetite and energy balance. Leptin, produced by fat cells, acts as a satiety signal, inhibiting hunger and reducing food intake when energy stores are sufficient. In contrast, ghrelin, secreted primarily by the stomach, stimulates appetite and promotes food intake, signaling the brain to increase hunger when energy levels are low.

Other hormones, such as cortisol and adrenaline, are released in response to stress or physical activity, mobilizing energy reserves and increasing metabolism to meet the body's demands. These hormones play a crucial role in the fight-or-flight response, enhancing alertness, increasing heart rate, and mobilizing glucose and fatty acids for energy production. Hormones like growth hormone and testosterone influence muscle growth, protein synthesis, and fat metabolism. Adequate sleep, proper nutrition, and regular exercise can help optimize the secretion of these hormones, promoting muscle development, fat loss, and overall metabolic health.

By understanding the role of hormones in metabolic responses, individuals can adopt lifestyle strategies to support hormonal balance and optimize metabolic function. This may include consuming a balanced diet, engaging in regular physical activity, managing stress levels, and prioritizing quality sleep. Moreover, targeted interventions such as intermittent fasting, carbohydrate cycling, and resistance training can further modulate hormonal responses to promote fat loss, muscle growth, and overall well-being.

Comparative Analysis: Metabolic Confusion vs. Traditional Diets

In comparing Metabolic Confusion to traditional diets, it's essential to understand the underlying principles and mechanisms driving each approach. Traditional diets often focus on restricting calories, macronutrients, or food groups to induce weight loss or improve health outcomes. These diets typically involve a static meal plan or eating pattern, often leading to metabolic adaptation and plateauing results over time. In contrast, Metabolic Confusion emphasizes variability and flexibility, cycling through different calorie intakes, macronutrient compositions, and meal timings to prevent metabolic adaptation and stimulate continuous progress. By strategically alternating between periods of higher and lower calorie intake, varying macronutrient ratios, and incorporating intermittent fasting or carbohydrate cycling, Metabolic Confusion aims to keep the body guessing and maintain metabolic flexibility. This approach not only enhances fat loss but also promotes metabolic health, hormone balance, and sustainability. Additionally, Metabolic Confusion encourages individualization and experimentation, allowing individuals to tailor their nutrition and lifestyle strategies based on personal preferences, goals, and metabolic responses. Overall, while traditional diets may offer short-term results, Metabolic Confusion provides a more dynamic and adaptable approach to long-term weight management and metabolic optimization.

What Sets Metabolic Confusion Apart?

Unlike traditional diets that often follow a rigid structure, Metabolic Confusion employs a flexible and dynamic strategy to keep the body constantly challenged and responsive. This approach involves cycling through different calorie levels, macronutrient compositions, meal timings, and even fasting protocols to prevent metabolic adaptation and plateauing. By continuously varying these factors, Metabolic Confusion aims to keep the body guessing and maintain metabolic flexibility, ultimately leading to sustained fat loss and improved metabolic health.

Another key aspect that sets Metabolic Confusion apart is its focus on individualization. Rather than prescribing a one-size-fits-all approach, Metabolic Confusion encourages individuals to tailor their nutrition and lifestyle strategies based on their unique needs, preferences, and metabolic responses. This personalized approach allows for greater adherence and long-term success, as individuals are more likely to stick to a plan that aligns with their individual goals and preferences. Metabolic Confusion places a strong emphasis on sustainability and lifestyle integration. Instead of relying on short-term fixes or extreme measures, Metabolic Confusion promotes sustainable habits that can be maintained over the long term. By incorporating a variety of foods, flavors, and eating patterns, individuals can enjoy a diverse and satisfying diet while still achieving their weight loss and health goals.

By embracing variability, individualization, and sustainability, Metabolic Confusion offers a refreshing alternative to traditional diets and provides a pathway to long-term success and metabolic optimization.

Studies and Evidence Supporting Metabolic Confusion

Studies and evidence supporting Metabolic Confusion as an effective dietary strategy abound, demonstrating its potential to enhance weight loss, improve metabolic health, and promote overall well-being. Research has consistently shown that the principles underlying Metabolic Confusion, such as calorie cycling, macronutrient rotation, and intermittent fasting, can yield significant benefits for individuals seeking to optimize their metabolism and achieve sustainable fat loss.

Numerous studies have highlighted the efficacy of calorie cycling in promoting weight loss while preserving metabolic rate and lean body mass. By alternating between periods of calorie restriction and maintenance or surplus, Metabolic Confusion helps prevent metabolic adaptation, allowing individuals to continue burning fat and maintaining a higher metabolic rate over time. This approach has been shown to be more effective than traditional continuous calorie restriction diets in achieving long-term weight loss and preventing weight regain. The metabolic benefits of macronutrient rotation, whereby individuals vary their intake of carbohydrates, proteins, and fats over time. This strategy can help prevent metabolic adaptation and insulin resistance, improve nutrient partitioning, and enhance metabolic flexibility. Studies have shown that alternating between high-carbohydrate and low-carbohydrate days, for example, can improve insulin sensitivity, enhance fat oxidation, and support weight loss efforts.

Intermittent fasting, another key component of Metabolic Confusion, has also been extensively studied for its metabolic and health benefits. Research indicates that intermittent fasting protocols, such as alternate-day fasting, time-restricted feeding, or periodic fasting, can promote weight loss, improve insulin sensitivity, reduce inflammation, and enhance cellular repair and rejuvenation. These fasting strategies help induce a state of mild metabolic stress, triggering beneficial physiological adaptations that support fat loss and metabolic health.

Studies have also investigated the psychological and behavioral aspects of Metabolic Confusion, demonstrating its potential to improve adherence and long-term sustainability. By incorporating flexibility, variety, and enjoyment into the dietary approach, Metabolic Confusion can help individuals overcome feelings of deprivation, boredom, or monotony often associated with traditional dieting. This can lead to greater compliance, satisfaction, and overall well-being, ultimately supporting successful weight management and metabolic optimization.

The body of scientific evidence supporting Metabolic Confusion continues to grow, highlighting its potential as a practical, effective, and sustainable approach to weight loss and metabolic health. By incorporating principles of variability, individualization, and flexibility, Metabolic Confusion offers a promising strategy for achieving lasting results and optimizing overall well-being.

The Impact of Macronutrient Variation

The impact of macronutrient variation on metabolic health and weight management is a key aspect of the Metabolic Confusion approach. By strategically rotating the intake of carbohydrates, proteins, and fats, Metabolic Confusion aims to optimize metabolic flexibility, enhance fat loss, and improve overall well-being.

Research has demonstrated that varying macronutrient intake can have profound effects on metabolism and physiological responses. For example, alternating between high-carbohydrate and low-carbohydrate days can help regulate insulin levels, improve insulin sensitivity, and enhance fat oxidation. This variation in carbohydrate intake can also support glycogen depletion and promote metabolic adaptation, leading to more efficient fat loss and weight management.

Similarly, rotating protein intake can impact satiety, muscle protein synthesis, and thermogenesis. Higher protein intake has been associated with increased feelings of fullness, greater preservation of lean body mass during weight loss, and improved metabolic rate. By cycling protein intake, individuals can optimize muscle protein synthesis, support muscle growth and repair, and enhance overall metabolic function. Varying fat intake can influence hormone production, lipid metabolism, and energy utilization. While fats are essential for hormone production, cell membrane integrity, and nutrient absorption, excessive fat intake can contribute to weight gain and metabolic dysfunction. By cycling fat intake, individuals can maintain adequate fat intake for optimal health while also supporting fat loss and metabolic flexibility.

Strategic variation of macronutrient intake within the Metabolic Confusion approach offers numerous metabolic benefits. By cycling carbohydrates, proteins, and fats, individuals can optimize insulin sensitivity, support muscle growth and repair, enhance fat oxidation, and promote overall metabolic health. This approach not only enhances weight loss and body composition but also supports long-term metabolic flexibility and well-being.

Carbohydrates, Proteins, and Fats: Rotating Your Macros

Rotating macronutrients—carbohydrates, proteins, and fats—is a cornerstone of the Metabolic Confusion approach, offering a dynamic way to optimize metabolism and support sustainable weight loss. By strategically alternating the intake of these macronutrients, individuals can harness their metabolic flexibility and promote various physiological responses conducive to fat loss and overall well-being.

Carbohydrates serve as the body's primary source of energy, but excessive intake, particularly of refined carbohydrates, can lead to spikes in blood sugar levels and insulin resistance. By cycling carbohydrate intake, individuals can regulate insulin levels, enhance fat oxidation, and improve metabolic flexibility. On high-carbohydrate days, emphasis can be placed on consuming complex carbohydrates from sources like whole grains, fruits, and vegetables, providing sustained energy and supporting glycogen replenishment. On low-carbohydrate days, the focus shifts to minimizing carbohydrate intake, which can promote ketosis, increase fat burning, and improve insulin sensitivity.

Proteins are essential for muscle repair, growth, and overall metabolic function. Adequate protein intake is crucial for preserving lean muscle mass during weight loss, promoting satiety, and supporting various metabolic processes. By rotating protein intake, individuals can optimize muscle protein synthesis, enhance satiety, and support metabolic rate. On higher protein days, emphasis can be placed on consuming lean protein sources such as poultry, fish, tofu, and legumes, ensuring adequate protein intake for muscle repair and growth. On lower protein days, protein intake can be moderated, allowing for greater flexibility in macronutrient distribution while still meeting daily protein needs.

Fats play a vital role in hormone production, cell membrane integrity, and nutrient absorption. While fats are calorie-dense, they also provide a sense of satiety and can support stable blood sugar levels. By rotating fat intake, individuals can optimize hormone production, support brain health, and enhance fat metabolism. On higher fat days, emphasis can be placed on consuming healthy fats from sources like avocados, nuts, seeds, and fatty fish, providing essential fatty acids and promoting satiety. On lower fat days, fat intake can be moderated, allowing for greater flexibility in overall calorie intake while still ensuring adequate fat intake for optimal health.

Rotating macronutrients within the Metabolic Confusion approach offers a flexible and effective strategy for optimizing metabolism, promoting fat loss, and supporting overall health and well-being. By strategically alternating carbohydrate, protein, and fat intake, individuals can harness their metabolic flexibility, enhance fat oxidation, and achieve sustainable results in their weight loss journey.

Timing and Quantity: How to Adjust Your Macronutrients Effectively

Adjusting macronutrients effectively involves careful consideration of both timing and quantity to optimize metabolic responses and support individual health and fitness goals. Timing refers to the distribution of macronutrients throughout the day, while quantity pertains to the amount consumed at each meal or snack. By understanding how to adjust both timing and quantity, individuals can better regulate blood sugar levels, enhance satiety, and support overall metabolic function.

When it comes to timing, it's essential to consider the body's natural circadian rhythm and metabolic response to food. For instance, consuming a balanced meal rich in protein, healthy fats, and complex carbohydrates within an hour of waking can help kickstart metabolism, stabilize blood sugar levels, and provide sustained energy throughout the day. Similarly, spacing meals and snacks evenly throughout the day can help maintain stable blood sugar levels and prevent excessive hunger or overeating later in the day. Additionally, adjusting macronutrient timing based on activity level can optimize performance and recovery, such as consuming carbohydrates and protein before and after exercise to support energy production and muscle repair.

In terms of quantity, portion control is key to ensuring adequate nutrient intake without overeating. Understanding individual calorie needs based on factors like age, gender, weight, activity level, and metabolic rate is crucial for determining appropriate portion sizes. Using tools like food scales, measuring cups, and nutrition labels can help accurately assess portion sizes and prevent unintentional overconsumption of calories and macronutrients. Additionally, balancing macronutrient intake at each meal and snack—such as including a source of protein, healthy fats, and carbohydrates—can help promote satiety, stabilize blood sugar levels, and support overall metabolic health.

Flexibility and adaptability are also important principles when adjusting macronutrients effectively. While general guidelines can provide a framework for macronutrient distribution, individual preferences, dietary restrictions, and lifestyle factors should also be taken into account. Experimenting with different macronutrient ratios, meal timing strategies, and portion sizes can help individuals find an approach that works best for their unique needs and goals. Regular monitoring of progress and adjustments as needed can help ensure continued success and long-term adherence to a balanced and sustainable nutrition plan.

Psychological Aspects of Metabolic Confusion

The psychological aspects of metabolic confusion play a crucial role in its effectiveness as a dietary approach. Unlike traditional diets that often involve strict rules and restrictions, metabolic confusion offers a more flexible and sustainable way of eating, which can positively impact an individual's mindset and relationship with food. By focusing on variety, flexibility, and balance, metabolic confusion promotes a sense of empowerment and autonomy over one's dietary choices, leading to improved adherence and long-term success.

One of the key psychological benefits of metabolic confusion is its ability to reduce feelings of deprivation and monotony commonly associated with traditional dieting. By rotating macronutrients, varying food choices, and incorporating a wide range of flavors and textures, metabolic confusion keeps meals exciting and enjoyable, preventing boredom and monotony. This can help individuals stay motivated and engaged with their dietary plan, making it easier to sustain over time.

The flexibility inherent in metabolic confusion allows individuals to adapt their eating patterns to fit their preferences, lifestyle, and social situations. Unlike rigid diet plans that dictate what and when to eat, metabolic confusion provides guidelines that can be customized to meet individual needs and goals. This flexibility reduces feelings of guilt or failure associated with deviating from a strict diet, empowering individuals to make informed choices that align with their values and preferences.

Another psychological benefit of metabolic confusion is its focus on overall health and well-being rather than just weight loss. By emphasizing nutrient-dense foods, balanced meals, and mindful eating practices, metabolic confusion promotes a holistic approach to health that goes beyond the number on the scale. This shift in mindset can help individuals develop a more positive relationship with food and their bodies, fostering feelings of self-confidence, empowerment, and self-worth. The adaptive nature of metabolic confusion encourages individuals to listen to their body's hunger and satiety cues, rather than relying on external rules or restrictions. This intuitive approach to eating promotes mindfulness and self-awareness, allowing individuals to develop a deeper understanding of their body's nutritional needs and preferences. As a result, individuals may experience greater satisfaction and enjoyment from their meals, leading to improved overall well-being and quality of life.

The psychological aspects of metabolic confusion are integral to its success as a dietary approach. By promoting flexibility, variety, and balance, metabolic confusion empowers individuals to take control of their eating habits, leading to improved adherence, satisfaction, and long-term success in achieving their health and wellness goals.

Avoiding Dietary Monotony: Psychological Benefits

Avoiding dietary monotony offers numerous psychological benefits that contribute to overall well-being and adherence to a dietary plan. Monotony in dieting often leads to boredom and dissatisfaction, making it challenging to maintain healthy eating habits over the long term. However, by incorporating variety and diversity into meals, individuals can experience several positive psychological outcomes.

Firstly, avoiding dietary monotony can enhance enjoyment and satisfaction with food. When meals are repetitive and lack variety, individuals may become disinterested in eating, leading to feelings of dissatisfaction and even resentment towards their diet. Conversely, incorporating a diverse range of flavors, textures, and ingredients can stimulate the senses and make eating a more pleasurable and enjoyable experience. This enjoyment can lead to greater satisfaction with meals, improving overall mood and well-being.

Additionally, avoiding dietary monotony promotes a positive relationship with food and eating. When individuals have access to a variety of nutritious and delicious foods, they are more likely to view food as a source of nourishment and pleasure rather than a source of restriction or deprivation. This positive relationship with food can help individuals develop healthier attitudes and behaviors around eating, reducing the risk of disordered eating patterns and promoting a balanced approach to nutrition.

Moreover, avoiding dietary monotony can support psychological well-being by reducing feelings of deprivation and restriction. Traditional diets often rely on rigid meal plans and strict rules, which can lead to feelings of deprivation and resentment towards certain foods. In contrast, a varied and diverse diet allows individuals to enjoy a wide range of foods without feeling restricted or deprived. This freedom to choose and enjoy foods can reduce stress and anxiety around eating, leading to improved psychological well-being and overall quality of life.

Furthermore, avoiding dietary monotony can promote mindfulness and present-moment awareness during meals. When individuals are exposed to a variety of flavors and textures, they are more likely to pay attention to the sensory experience of eating, such as taste, smell, and texture. This mindfulness can help individuals develop a deeper appreciation for food and eating, leading to greater satisfaction and enjoyment with meals.

Overall, avoiding dietary monotony offers numerous psychological benefits that can enhance overall well-being and adherence to a healthy eating plan. By incorporating variety and diversity into meals, individuals can experience greater enjoyment, satisfaction, and mindfulness with their food, leading to improved psychological well-being and long-term success in maintaining healthy eating habits.

Strategies for Staying Motivated on a Varied Diet Plan

Staying motivated on a varied diet plan can be challenging, but there are several strategies that can help individuals maintain their enthusiasm and commitment to healthy eating habits. One effective strategy is to set realistic and achievable goals. By setting specific, measurable, and attainable goals, individuals can track their progress and celebrate their successes along the way, which can help to boost motivation and confidence. Additionally, incorporating variety into meals can help to prevent boredom and monotony, making it easier to stick to a healthy eating plan. Trying new recipes, exploring different cuisines, and experimenting with diverse ingredients can keep meals exciting and enjoyable, helping individuals stay motivated to continue making nutritious choices.

Another strategy for staying motivated on a varied diet plan is to focus on the benefits of healthy eating. Reminding oneself of the positive impact that nutritious foods have on overall health and well-being can provide motivation to make healthy choices, even when faced with temptations or obstacles. Whether it's increased energy levels, improved mood, or better physical health, focusing on the benefits of healthy eating can help individuals stay committed to their dietary goals.

Finding social support can be instrumental in staying motivated on a varied diet plan. Connecting with friends, family members, or online communities who share similar health goals can provide encouragement, accountability, and motivation to stay on track. Sharing successes, challenges, and experiences with others can help individuals feel supported and motivated to continue making healthy choices.

Practicing self-care and managing stress are also important strategies for staying motivated on a varied diet plan. Taking time to prioritize sleep, relaxation, and stress-reduction activities can help individuals maintain the mental and emotional resilience needed to stick to their dietary goals, even during challenging times. Engaging in activities such as yoga, meditation, or spending time outdoors can help individuals manage stress levels and maintain a positive mindset, making it easier to stay motivated to eat healthily.

Celebrating progress and rewarding oneself for sticking to a varied diet plan can help maintain motivation over the long term. Whether it's treating oneself to a small indulgence, enjoying a favorite activity, or simply acknowledging one's achievements, celebrating milestones along the way can provide a sense of accomplishment and motivation to continue making healthy choices. By implementing these strategies and staying focused on their goals, individuals can stay motivated and committed to their varied diet plan, ultimately achieving long-term success in maintaining a healthy lifestyle.

CHAPTER 2

BODY TYPES

Understanding Body Types: An Overview

Understanding body types is essential for tailoring fitness and nutrition plans to individual needs and goals. While every person is unique, body types are generally categorized into three main classifications: ectomorph, mesomorph, and endomorph.

Ectomorphs typically have a slender build with narrow shoulders and hips, and they often struggle to gain weight or muscle mass. They tend to have a fast metabolism, which means they may find it challenging to put on size despite eating a lot. Ectomorphs may benefit from focusing on strength training to build muscle and incorporating calorie-dense foods into their diet to support weight gain.

Mesomorphs are characterized by a naturally athletic and muscular physique, with broad shoulders, a narrow waist, and well-defined muscles. They tend to respond well to both strength training and cardiovascular exercise, making it easier for them to build muscle and maintain a lean physique. Mesomorphs typically have a balanced metabolism and may benefit from a combination of resistance training and cardiovascular exercise to support overall fitness and body composition goals.

Endomorphs typically have a larger frame with a higher percentage of body fat and a slower metabolism. They may find it easier to gain weight, especially in the form of fat, and may struggle to lose weight despite diet and exercise efforts. Endomorphs may benefit from focusing on both strength training and high-intensity interval training (HIIT) to boost metabolism and promote fat loss. Additionally, paying attention to portion control and eating a balanced diet rich in whole foods can help support weight management goals for endomorphs.

It's important to note that these classifications are generalizations, and many individuals may fall somewhere in between two body types or exhibit characteristics of more than one type. Additionally, factors such as genetics, age, gender, and lifestyle habits can all influence body composition and metabolism. By understanding their body type, individuals can better tailor their fitness and nutrition strategies to optimize their results and achieve their health and wellness goals.

The Concept of Somatotypes

The concept of somatotypes, introduced by psychologist William Herbert Sheldon in the 1940s, suggests that individuals can be classified into three primary body types based on their physical characteristics and tendencies. These body types are known as ectomorph, mesomorph, and endomorph.

Ectomorphs are typically characterized by a lean and slender build, with narrow shoulders and hips, and longer limbs. They tend to have a fast metabolism, which makes it challenging for them to gain weight or muscle mass. Ectomorphs often have difficulty putting on muscle despite their best efforts and may need to consume a higher caloric diet with a focus on nutrient-dense foods to support weight gain and muscle growth.

Mesomorphs, on the other hand, are often described as naturally athletic and muscular individuals with a well-defined physique. They typically have broad shoulders, a narrow waist, and a high muscle-to-fat ratio. Mesomorphs tend to respond well to both strength training and cardiovascular exercise, making it easier for them to build muscle and maintain a lean physique. They often have a balanced metabolism and may find it easier to achieve their fitness and body composition goals compared to other body types.

Endomorphs are characterized by a larger and more rounded physique, with a higher percentage of body fat and a slower metabolism. They may have a wider frame, with a tendency to store excess fat in areas such as the abdomen and thighs. Endomorphs often struggle to lose weight and may find it challenging to maintain a lean body composition despite their efforts. They may benefit from a combination of strength training and high-intensity interval training (HIIT) to boost metabolism and promote fat loss, along with a balanced diet focused on portion control and nutrient-dense foods.

It's important to recognize that while somatotypes provide a framework for understanding body types, most individuals do not fit neatly into one category and may exhibit characteristics of multiple somatotypes to varying degrees. Additionally, factors such as genetics, age, gender, and lifestyle habits can all influence body composition and metabolism. By understanding their somatotype, individuals can better tailor their fitness and nutrition strategies to optimize their results and achieve their health and wellness goals.

Recognizing Your Body Type: Physical and Metabolic Traits

Recognizing your body type involves understanding both your physical characteristics and metabolic traits. Physical traits include aspects like bone structure, muscle mass, and body fat distribution, while metabolic traits encompass factors such as metabolism speed, insulin sensitivity, and how your body responds to different types of exercise and nutrition.

One common way to categorize body types is through the concept of somatotypes, which classifies individuals into three primary categories: ectomorph, mesomorph, and endomorph. Ectomorphs typically have a lean and slender build, mesomorphs are naturally athletic and muscular, and endomorphs tend to have a larger, more rounded physique with higher body fat levels. Beyond somatotypes, recognizing your body type involves understanding how your body responds to various stimuli. For example, some people may have a fast metabolism that allows them to burn calories quickly, while others may have a slower metabolism that makes weight management more challenging. Similarly, some individuals may have higher insulin sensitivity, while others may be more prone to insulin resistance, which can affect how their bodies process carbohydrates and manage blood sugar levels.

By recognizing your body type, both in terms of physical characteristics and metabolic traits, you can better tailor your fitness and nutrition approach to support your health and wellness goals. Understanding how your body responds to different types of exercise and dietary patterns can help you make informed choices that support optimal performance, body composition, and overall well-being.

The Endomorph Profile: Characteristics and Challenges

Endomorphs typically exhibit certain physical and metabolic characteristics that distinguish them from other body types. Physically, they often have a rounder or softer appearance, with a tendency to store excess fat, particularly around the abdomen, hips, and thighs. They may also have a larger bone structure and a more substantial overall build compared to ectomorphs or mesomorphs.

Metabolically, endomorphs may face challenges related to slower metabolism and insulin sensitivity. This combination can make it easier for them to gain weight, especially if they consume excess calories or follow a diet high in refined carbohydrates and sugars. They may also struggle with managing blood sugar levels, which can increase the risk of conditions like type 2 diabetes and metabolic syndrome.

Due to these characteristics, endomorphs often find it more challenging to lose weight and maintain a lean physique compared to other body types. However, it's essential to recognize that everyone's body is unique, and individual responses to diet and exercise can vary widely, even within the same somatotype category.

Despite the potential challenges, endomorphs can still achieve their health and fitness goals with the right approach. Strategies such as focusing on whole, nutrient-dense foods, controlling portion sizes, and incorporating regular physical activity, including both cardiovascular exercise and strength training, can help support weight management and overall health.

Paying attention to factors like stress management, adequate sleep, and hydration can also play a crucial role in optimizing metabolic health and supporting a balanced lifestyle. By understanding their unique characteristics and challenges, endomorphs can develop personalized strategies to improve their overall well-being and achieve their desired health and fitness outcomes.

Common Traits of Endomorphs

Endomorphs, characterized by a softer, rounder body shape and a tendency to store excess body fat, often exhibit several common physical and metabolic traits. These traits can provide insights into their body composition, metabolism, and potential response to diet and exercise interventions. Here are some common traits of endomorphs:

1. Higher Body Fat Percentage: Endomorphs typically have a higher percentage of body fat compared to other body types, particularly around the abdomen, hips, and thighs. They may have a rounder or softer appearance and struggle to achieve a lean physique.

2. Slower Metabolism: Endomorphs often have a slower metabolism, which can make it easier to gain weight and harder to lose it. Their bodies may be more efficient at storing energy as fat, leading to challenges in weight management and body composition.

3. Difficulty Losing Weight: Endomorphs may find it challenging to lose weight, especially when compared to ectomorphs or mesomorphs. Their bodies may resist fat loss efforts, making it necessary to adopt a comprehensive approach that includes both dietary modifications and regular exercise.

4. Carb Sensitivity: Endomorphs may be more sensitive to carbohydrates, particularly refined carbohydrates and sugars, which can lead to spikes in blood sugar levels and increased fat storage. Managing carbohydrate intake and focusing on complex carbohydrates, fiber-rich foods, and balanced meals can help regulate blood sugar levels and support weight management.

5. Tendency to Store Fat Easily: Endomorphs have a natural propensity to store fat, particularly in the abdominal region. Hormonal factors, such as insulin resistance and cortisol levels, may contribute to increased fat storage and difficulty in mobilizing stored fat for energy.

6. Challenges Building Muscle Definition: While endomorphs may have a higher potential for muscle mass due to their larger frame and higher fat-free mass, they may struggle to achieve muscle definition and a lean, toned appearance. Resistance training and cardiovascular exercise can help improve muscle tone and overall body composition.

7. Preference for High-Calorie Foods: Endomorphs may have a preference for high-calorie or comfort foods, which can contribute to overeating and weight gain. Adopting mindful eating practices, such as paying attention to hunger and fullness cues, and choosing nutrient-dense, whole foods can help support weight management goals.

8. Thrive in Endurance Activities: Despite challenges in weight management, endomorphs may excel in endurance activities that utilize their natural stamina and energy reserves. Engaging in regular cardiovascular exercise, such as walking, cycling, or swimming, can help improve fitness levels and support overall health.

Understanding these common traits of endomorphs can help individuals with this body type tailor their diet, exercise, and lifestyle strategies to support their unique needs and goals. By adopting a holistic approach that addresses both physical and metabolic characteristics, endomorphs can optimize their health, fitness, and well-being.

Metabolic Implications: Why Weight Management Can Be Challenging

Weight management can present significant challenges, particularly for individuals with certain metabolic profiles. Several metabolic implications contribute to the complexity of weight management. Firstly, variations in metabolic rate among individuals can affect how efficiently calories are burned, making it easier for some to gain weight and harder for others to lose it. Additionally, hormonal imbalances, such as insulin resistance or thyroid dysfunction, can disrupt metabolic processes and lead to weight gain or difficulty losing weight. Genetic factors play a role in determining an individual's susceptibility to weight gain and their body's response to dietary and lifestyle interventions. Environmental factors like stress, sleep deprivation, and sedentary behavior further complicate weight management efforts by influencing appetite, cravings, and energy expenditure. Understanding these metabolic implications is essential for developing personalized weight management strategies that address the underlying factors contributing to weight gain and promote sustainable lifestyle changes.

Overall, the fast metabolism and lean body composition of ectomorphs present unique challenges for weight management and muscle gain. By adopting a balanced approach that includes regular strength training, caloric-dense foods, and adequate rest and recovery, ectomorphs can overcome these challenges and achieve their weight and fitness goals effectively. Working with a registered dietitian or fitness professional can provide personalized guidance and support to optimize their nutritional intake and exercise regimen for optimal results.

The Mesomorph and Ectomorph: A Comparative Analysis

The Mesomorph and Ectomorph body types represent two distinct categories with unique characteristics and metabolic profiles, each influencing how individuals respond to diet, exercise, and weight management strategies. A comparative analysis of these body types sheds light on their differences and provides valuable insights into tailoring effective wellness approaches.

Mesomorphs are typically characterized by a muscular and athletic build, with well-defined muscles and a naturally higher metabolic rate. They tend to have an easier time gaining muscle mass and strength compared to other body types. Mesomorphs often excel in activities requiring power, strength, and speed, such as weightlifting, sprinting, and contact sports. From a metabolic perspective, mesomorphs typically have a more efficient metabolism, allowing them to burn calories more effectively and maintain a lean physique with relative ease. However, this metabolic advantage can also predispose mesomorphs to weight gain if they consume excess calories or lead a sedentary lifestyle.

In contrast, ectomorphs are characterized by a lean and slender physique, with long limbs and minimal body fat. They often struggle to gain muscle mass and may have a fast metabolism that makes it challenging to gain weight, even when consuming a high-calorie diet. Ectomorphs may find it difficult to build muscle and strength compared to mesomorphs, but they may excel in endurance-based activities such as long-distance running or cycling. Despite their metabolic advantage in terms of calorie burning, ectomorphs may face challenges in maintaining muscle mass and achieving a muscular appearance.

Understanding the metabolic differences between mesomorphs and ectomorphs is essential for developing tailored nutrition and exercise plans that align with their specific goals and challenges. For mesomorphs, focusing on strength training and consuming a balanced diet with adequate protein can help support muscle growth and maintenance while managing body fat levels. Ectomorphs may benefit from a higher calorie intake and emphasis on resistance training to stimulate muscle growth and enhance their physique.

While mesomorphs and ectomorphs may have different metabolic profiles and body compositions, both can achieve their health and fitness goals with the right approach. By leveraging their unique strengths and addressing their specific challenges, individuals of all body types can optimize their metabolic health and achieve long-term success in their wellness journey.

Mesomorphs: Balanced and Muscular

Mesomorphs are often described as the balanced body type, combining elements of both endomorphs and ectomorphs. They typically exhibit a naturally muscular and athletic physique, with well-defined muscles, broad shoulders, and a narrow waist. Mesomorphs tend to have a moderate metabolism, allowing them to build muscle mass relatively easily while maintaining a lean body composition.

One of the key characteristics of mesomorphs is their ability to respond favorably to both strength training and cardiovascular exercise. They have a genetic predisposition to gain muscle mass and strength efficiently, making them well-suited for activities such as weightlifting, bodybuilding, and powerlifting. Additionally, mesomorphs often excel in sports that require a combination of strength, speed, and agility, such as sprinting, gymnastics, and martial arts.

From a metabolic standpoint, mesomorphs typically have a balanced energy expenditure, meaning they burn calories at a moderate rate and can maintain their weight with relative ease. However, this doesn't mean they can neglect their diet or exercise regimen. While mesomorphs may have a genetic advantage when it comes to building muscle and staying lean, they still need to prioritize proper nutrition and regular physical activity to optimize their health and fitness.

In terms of dietary recommendations, mesomorphs may benefit from a balanced macronutrient intake, including adequate protein to support muscle growth and repair, healthy fats for hormone regulation and energy, and complex carbohydrates for sustained energy levels. Additionally, incorporating a variety of nutrient-dense foods, such as fruits, vegetables, whole grains, and lean proteins, can help mesomorphs maintain their overall health and performance.

Mesomorphs are blessed with a combination of muscle mass, strength, and metabolic balance that can set them up for success in their fitness journey. By capitalizing on their genetic advantages and adopting a balanced approach to nutrition and exercise, mesomorphs can achieve their health and fitness goals while maintaining their muscular and athletic physique.

Ectomorphs: Lean and Fast-Metabolizing

Ectomorphs are characterized by their naturally lean and slender physique, with long limbs, narrow shoulders, and a fast metabolism. These individuals often find it challenging to gain weight, including both muscle and fat, despite consuming a high-calorie diet. Ectomorphs typically have a higher metabolic rate, meaning they burn calories at a faster pace than other body types, which can make it difficult for them to build muscle mass and maintain a healthy weight.

One of the defining features of ectomorphs is their ability to stay relatively lean, even when consuming large amounts of food. While this may seem like an advantage, it can pose challenges for those looking to increase muscle size and strength. Ectomorphs often need to consume a higher calorie intake and focus on strength training exercises to stimulate muscle growth and development.

From a metabolic standpoint, ectomorphs have a higher proportion of fast-twitch muscle fibers, which are more suited for endurance activities rather than explosive power. As a result, they may excel in sports that require sustained energy output over long periods, such as distance running, cycling, or swimming. However, they may struggle in activities that require short bursts of power and strength, such as weightlifting or sprinting.

In terms of dietary recommendations, ectomorphs may benefit from a higher calorie intake consisting of nutrient-dense foods to support their metabolism and energy needs. This includes a balanced macronutrient ratio of carbohydrates, proteins, and fats, with an emphasis on complex carbohydrates to provide sustained energy throughout the day. Additionally, incorporating resistance training exercises into their workout routine can help ectomorphs build muscle mass and increase strength over time.

Despite the challenges they may face in gaining weight and building muscle, ectomorphs can still achieve their fitness goals with patience, consistency, and the right approach to nutrition and exercise. By understanding their unique metabolic profile and tailoring their diet and training regimen accordingly, ectomorphs can optimize their health and performance while embracing their lean and fast-metabolizing physique.

CHAPTER 3

THE 28-DAY MEAL PLAN OVERVIEW

Introduction to the 28-Day Cycle

Welcome to Chapter 3, where we delve into the comprehensive overview of the 28-Day Meal Plan. This meticulously crafted plan is designed to guide you through a transformative journey towards a healthier lifestyle. Over the next four weeks, you'll embark on a nutritional adventure, exploring a diverse array of delicious recipes and strategically curated meals to fuel your body and nourish your soul.

The 28-Day Cycle is structured to provide you with a systematic approach to nutrition, incorporating principles of metabolic confusion to optimize your metabolism and support your weight loss goals. Each week of the cycle is carefully planned to introduce variation in calorie intake, macronutrient composition, and meal timing, ensuring that your body remains responsive and adaptable throughout the program.

As you progress through the 28-Day Cycle, you'll experience a gradual evolution in your dietary habits and metabolic function. By embracing the principles of metabolic confusion, you'll learn how to harness the power of strategic variation to stimulate fat loss, preserve lean muscle mass, and enhance overall metabolic flexibility. This approach not only promotes sustainable weight loss but also fosters a deeper understanding of your body's unique nutritional needs and metabolic responses.

Throughout the 28-Day Cycle, you'll have the opportunity to explore a wide range of flavorful and nutritious recipes, carefully crafted to tantalize your taste buds and nourish your body from within. From energizing breakfast options to satisfying dinners and everything in between, each meal is thoughtfully designed to provide optimal nutrition while satisfying your cravings and keeping you feeling satisfied.

So whether you're looking to kickstart your weight loss journey, revitalize your metabolism, or simply adopt healthier eating habits, the 28-Day Meal Plan offers a comprehensive roadmap to help you achieve your goals. Get ready to embark on a transformative culinary adventure and discover the power of metabolic confusion to unlock your full potential for health and vitality.

Now, let's dive deeper into how metabolic confusion works and explore the myriad benefits of cycling your calorie intake, setting the stage for a successful and fulfilling journey towards a healthier, happier you.

How Metabolic Confusion Works

Metabolic confusion is a dietary strategy that involves varying calorie intake, macronutrient composition, and meal timing to promote metabolic flexibility and enhance weight loss. The concept is rooted in the idea that the body adapts to consistent patterns of eating, which can lead to plateaus in weight loss and metabolic slowdowns. By introducing variability into the diet, such as alternating between high and low-calorie days, rotating macronutrients, and changing meal timing, metabolic confusion aims to prevent the body from adapting to a specific eating pattern, thereby boosting metabolism and promoting fat loss.

One way metabolic confusion works is by preventing metabolic adaptation, where the body adjusts its energy expenditure and hormone levels in response to changes in calorie intake and physical activity. When calorie intake is consistently low, for example, the body may downregulate metabolic rate and conserve energy, making it harder to lose weight. By incorporating periodic high-calorie days or refeeds, metabolic confusion helps prevent this adaptive response, keeping the metabolism elevated and promoting fat burning.

Metabolic confusion may enhance nutrient partitioning, which refers to how the body utilizes nutrients for energy production, muscle building, and fat storage. By cycling macronutrients, such as alternating between high-carb and low-carb days or varying protein intake, metabolic confusion can optimize nutrient utilization and promote muscle growth while minimizing fat storage. This approach may also improve insulin sensitivity and hormone regulation, which are key factors in metabolic health and weight management.

Another mechanism by which metabolic confusion works is by promoting metabolic flexibility, which is the ability of the body to efficiently switch between different fuel sources, such as carbohydrates and fats, depending on dietary and metabolic demands. By varying meal timing and introducing periods of fasting or intermittent fasting, metabolic confusion can train the body to become more adaptable and efficient in using stored fat for fuel, thereby enhancing fat oxidation and supporting weight loss.

By disrupting the body's adaptation to a specific eating pattern, promoting metabolic flexibility, and optimizing nutrient partitioning to enhance fat loss and improve metabolic health. By incorporating variability into the diet and meal timing, individuals can harness the power of metabolic confusion to overcome weight loss plateaus, accelerate fat loss, and achieve their health and fitness goals.

Benefits of Cycling Your Calorie Intake

Cycling calorie intake, a key strategy in metabolic confusion, offers several benefits for weight loss and overall metabolic health. One significant advantage is that it prevents the body from adapting to a consistent calorie deficit, which can lead to metabolic slowdowns and plateaus in weight loss. By alternating between periods of higher and lower calorie intake, cycling calorie intake helps maintain a higher metabolic rate, preventing the body from downregulating energy expenditure in response to prolonged calorie restriction.

It can enhance nutrient partitioning, optimizing how the body utilizes nutrients for energy production, muscle building, and fat storage. By incorporating periods of higher calorie intake, individuals can support muscle growth and repair while minimizing the risk of muscle loss often associated with prolonged calorie restriction. This approach promotes a favorable body composition, with a higher proportion of lean muscle mass to fat mass, which is essential for metabolic health and weight management.

Another benefit of cycling calorie intake is improved adherence to the diet. By allowing for periods of higher calorie intake, individuals can enjoy their favorite foods and meals without feeling deprived or restricted. This flexibility makes the diet more sustainable in the long term, reducing the likelihood of binge eating or falling off track with the nutrition plan. Additionally, incorporating variety into the diet can help prevent boredom and monotony, making it easier to stick to the program and achieve weight loss goals.

Furthermore, cycling calorie intake can have positive effects on metabolic hormones, such as leptin and ghrelin, which regulate hunger, satiety, and energy balance. Periods of higher calorie intake can help normalize these hormones, reducing feelings of hunger and preventing overeating during periods of calorie restriction. This hormonal balance promotes greater adherence to the diet and facilitates weight loss by supporting a more favorable energy balance.

It offers several benefits for weight loss and metabolic health, including preventing metabolic adaptation, optimizing nutrient partitioning, improving adherence to the diet, and supporting hormonal balance. By incorporating periods of higher and lower calorie intake into the nutrition plan, individuals can harness the power of metabolic confusion to achieve their weight loss goals more effectively and sustainably.

CHAPTER 4

THE 28-DAY MEAL PLAN WITH RECIPES

WEEK 1
ESTABLISHING THE FOUNDATION

BREAKFAST
Day 1 to 7: Energizing Morning Starters

Avocado and Egg Toast
Ingredients:

- 1 ripe avocado
- 2 eggs
- 2 slices of whole grain bread
- Salt and pepper to taste

Directions:

1. Start by slicing the avocado in half and removing the pit. Scoop out the flesh into a bowl and mash it with a fork until smooth.
2. Toast the slices of whole grain bread until golden brown and crispy.
3. While the bread is toasting, heat a non-stick skillet over medium heat and crack the eggs into the pan.
4. Cook the eggs to your preference (poached, fried, or scrambled) until the whites are set but the yolks are still slightly runny.
5. Once the bread is toasted, spread the mashed avocado evenly onto each slice.
6. Carefully transfer the cooked eggs onto the avocado toast.
7. Season with salt and pepper to taste.
8. Serve immediately and enjoy this delicious and nutritious breakfast!

Nutritional Values (per serving):

- Calories: 320
- Fat: 18g
- Carbohydrates: 26g
- Protein: 15g

Greek Yogurt Parfait with Mixed Berries and Nuts
Ingredients:

- 1 cup Greek yogurt
- 1/2 cup mixed berries (such as strawberries, blueberries, raspberries)
- 1/4 cup chopped nuts (such as almonds, walnuts)
- Honey or maple syrup (optional)

Directions:

1. Start by layering Greek yogurt at the bottom of a glass or bowl.
2. Add a layer of mixed berries on top of the yogurt.
3. Sprinkle chopped nuts over the berries.

4. Repeat the layers until the glass or bowl is filled.
5. Drizzle honey or maple syrup over the top for added sweetness, if desired.
6. Serve immediately and enjoy this delicious and nutritious Greek yogurt parfait!

Nutritional Values (per serving):

- Calories: 250
- Fat: 12g
- Carbohydrates: 20g
- Protein: 18g

Spinach and Feta Omelette

Ingredients:

- 2 eggs
- Handful of fresh spinach leaves
- 1/4 cup crumbled feta cheese
- Salt and pepper to taste

Directions:

1. Crack the eggs into a bowl and whisk them together until well combined. Season with salt and pepper.
2. Heat a non-stick skillet over medium heat and add a splash of oil or butter.
3. Add the fresh spinach leaves to the skillet and cook until wilted, stirring occasionally.
4. Pour the beaten eggs over the spinach in the skillet, ensuring they cover the entire surface evenly.
5. Allow the eggs to cook undisturbed for a few minutes until the edges start to set.
6. Sprinkle the crumbled feta cheese evenly over one half of the omelette.
7. Carefully fold the other half of the omelette over the filling using a spatula.
8. Cook for another minute or two until the cheese melts and the eggs are fully cooked through.
9. Slide the omelette onto a plate and serve hot.

Nutritional Values (per serving):

- Calories: 220
- Fat: 16g
- Carbohydrates: 2g
- Protein: 16g

Banana Pancakes with Honey and Walnuts

Ingredients:

- 1 ripe banana, mashed
- 2 eggs
- 1/4 teaspoon cinnamon
- 1/4 cup chopped walnuts
- Honey for drizzling

Directions:

1. In a mixing bowl, mash the ripe banana until smooth.
2. Add the eggs and cinnamon to the mashed banana, and whisk until well combined.
3. Heat a non-stick skillet or griddle over medium heat and lightly grease with oil or butter.
4. Pour small portions of the batter onto the skillet to form pancakes.
5. Sprinkle chopped walnuts onto each pancake.
6. Cook for 2-3 minutes on each side, or until golden brown and cooked through.
7. Stack the pancakes on a plate and drizzle with honey.

8. Serve hot and enjoy this delightful breakfast treat!

Nutritional Values (per serving):

- Calories: 270
- Fat: 16g
- Carbohydrates: 26g
- Protein: 9g

Smoothie Bowl with Kale, Banana, and Protein Powder

Ingredients:

- 1 cup kale leaves, stems removed
- 1 ripe banana
- 1/2 cup Greek yogurt
- 1/2 cup almond milk (or any milk of choice)
- 1 scoop protein powder (optional)
- Toppings: sliced banana, granola, chia seeds, shredded coconut

Directions:

1. In a blender, combine the kale leaves, ripe banana, Greek yogurt, almond milk, and protein powder (if using).
2. Blend on high speed until smooth and creamy, adding more almond milk if needed to reach your desired consistency.
3. Pour the smoothie into a bowl.
4. Arrange your desired toppings, such as sliced banana, granola, chia seeds, and shredded coconut, on top of the smoothie bowl.
5. Serve immediately and enjoy this nutritious and delicious smoothie bowl!

Nutritional Values (per serving, without toppings):

- Calories: 250
- Fat: 3g
- Carbohydrates: 35g
- Protein: 21g

Cottage Cheese with Pineapple Chunks

Ingredients:

- 1/2 cup cottage cheese
- 1/2 cup pineapple chunks (fresh or canned, drained)
- Optional: honey or maple syrup for drizzling

Directions:

1. Spoon the cottage cheese into a bowl.
2. Add the pineapple chunks on top of the cottage cheese.
3. If desired, drizzle honey or maple syrup over the cottage cheese and pineapple.
4. Serve immediately and enjoy this simple and nutritious snack or breakfast option!

Nutritional Values (per serving):

- Calories: 160
- Fat: 2g
- Carbohydrates: 20g
- Protein: 16g

Scrambled Tofu with Turmeric and Tomatoes

Ingredients:

- 1 block (about 14 oz) firm tofu, drained and crumbled
- 1 tablespoon olive oil
- 1 teaspoon ground turmeric
- 1/2 teaspoon ground cumin
- 1/2 teaspoon paprika
- Salt and pepper to taste
- 1 cup cherry tomatoes, halved
- 2 green onions, chopped
- Fresh cilantro, chopped (for garnish)

Directions:

1. Heat olive oil in a non-stick skillet over medium heat.
2. Add crumbled tofu to the skillet and sprinkle with ground turmeric, ground cumin, paprika, salt, and pepper.
3. Cook tofu, stirring occasionally, for about 5-7 minutes or until it starts to brown slightly.
4. Add cherry tomatoes and chopped green onions to the skillet. Cook for another 2-3 minutes until the tomatoes are softened.
5. Taste and adjust seasoning if necessary.
6. Garnish with fresh chopped cilantro before serving.
7. Serve hot and enjoy this flavorful and nutritious scrambled tofu with turmeric and tomatoes!

Nutritional Values (per serving):

- Calories: 180
- Fat: 10g
- Carbohydrates: 8g
- Protein: 16g

LUNCH

Day 1 to 7: Nutritious Midday Meals

Quinoa Salad with Chickpeas and Roasted Vegetables

Ingredients:

- 1 cup quinoa, rinsed
- 2 cups water or vegetable broth
- 1 can (15 oz) chickpeas, drained and rinsed
- 2 cups mixed vegetables (such as bell peppers, zucchini, cherry tomatoes)
- 2 tablespoons olive oil
- Salt and pepper to taste
- 1/4 cup fresh parsley, chopped
- Juice of 1 lemon

Directions:

1. Preheat the oven to 400°F (200°C).
2. In a saucepan, bring the water or vegetable broth to a boil. Add the quinoa, reduce heat to low, cover, and simmer for 15-20 minutes or until the quinoa is cooked and the liquid is absorbed. Remove from heat and let it cool.
3. Meanwhile, spread the mixed vegetables on a baking sheet. Drizzle with olive oil and season with salt and pepper. Toss to coat evenly.
4. Roast the vegetables in the preheated oven for 20-25 minutes or until they are tender and slightly caramelized.
5. In a large bowl, combine the cooked quinoa, roasted vegetables, and chickpeas.
6. Add chopped fresh parsley and squeeze lemon juice over the salad. Toss gently to combine.
7. Taste and adjust seasoning if necessary.
8. Serve the quinoa salad warm or chilled, and enjoy this nutritious and flavorful midday meal!

Nutritional Values (per serving):

- Calories: 320
- Fat: 10g
- Carbohydrates: 48g
- Protein: 12g

Turkey and Avocado Wrap

Ingredients:

- 1 large whole wheat tortilla or wrap
- 3-4 slices turkey breast

- 1/2 avocado, sliced
- 1/4 cup shredded lettuce
- 2 slices tomato
- 2 slices cucumber
- 1 tablespoon hummus or Greek yogurt spread (optional)
- Salt and pepper to taste

Directions:

1. Lay the whole wheat tortilla on a clean surface.
2. Spread hummus or Greek yogurt spread (if using) evenly over the tortilla, leaving about an inch border around the edges.
3. Layer the turkey breast slices, avocado slices, shredded lettuce, tomato slices, and cucumber slices over the tortilla, leaving some space at the bottom edge.
4. Season with salt and pepper to taste.
5. Starting from the bottom edge, tightly roll the tortilla into a wrap, folding in the sides as you go.
6. Secure the wrap with toothpicks if necessary.
7. Slice the wrap in half diagonally before serving, if desired.
8. Serve immediately, and enjoy this delicious and satisfying turkey and avocado wrap for lunch!

Nutritional Values (per serving):

- Calories: 350
- Fat: 14g
- Carbohydrates: 35g
- Protein: 22g

Grilled Chicken Salad with Balsamic Vinaigrette

Ingredients:

For the Salad:

- 2 boneless, skinless chicken breasts
- 6 cups mixed salad greens (such as lettuce, spinach, arugula)
- 1 cup cherry tomatoes, halved
- 1/2 cucumber, sliced
- 1/4 red onion, thinly sliced
- 1/4 cup crumbled feta cheese (optional)
- 1/4 cup chopped walnuts or almonds (optional)

For the Balsamic Vinaigrette:

- 3 tablespoons balsamic vinegar
- 2 tablespoons extra virgin olive oil
- 1 teaspoon Dijon mustard
- 1 clove garlic, minced
- Salt and pepper to taste

Directions:

1. Preheat grill or grill pan to medium-high heat.
2. Season the chicken breasts with salt and pepper.
3. Grill the chicken breasts for 6-7 minutes on each side, or until cooked through and no longer pink in the center. Remove from the grill and let them rest for a few minutes before slicing.
4. In a small bowl, whisk together the balsamic vinegar, olive oil, Dijon mustard, minced garlic, salt, and pepper to make the balsamic vinaigrette.
5. In a large salad bowl, combine the mixed salad greens, cherry tomatoes, cucumber slices, and thinly sliced red onion.
6. Slice the grilled chicken breasts and arrange them on top of the salad.

7. Drizzle the balsamic vinaigrette over the salad and toss gently to coat.
8. If desired, sprinkle crumbled feta cheese and chopped walnuts or almonds over the salad for extra flavor and texture.
9. Serve immediately and enjoy this delicious and nutritious grilled chicken salad with balsamic vinaigrette!

Nutritional Values (per serving, without optional toppings):

- Calories: 300
- Fat: 15g
- Carbohydrates: 10g
- Protein: 30g

Vegetable Stir-Fry with Brown Rice

Ingredients:

For the Stir-Fry:

- 2 cups cooked brown rice
- 2 tablespoons sesame oil
- 2 cloves garlic, minced
- 1 small onion, thinly sliced
- 1 bell pepper, thinly sliced
- 1 cup broccoli florets
- 1 cup sliced carrots
- 1 cup snap peas
- 1 cup sliced mushrooms
- 1/4 cup soy sauce (or tamari for gluten-free option)
- 1 tablespoon rice vinegar
- 1 tablespoon honey or maple syrup (optional)
- Sesame seeds for garnish (optional)
- Sliced green onions for garnish (optional)

Directions:

1. Heat sesame oil in a large skillet or wok over medium-high heat.
2. Add minced garlic and sliced onion to the skillet, and sauté for 2-3 minutes until fragrant and translucent.
3. Add bell pepper, broccoli florets, sliced carrots, snap peas, and sliced mushrooms to the skillet. Stir-fry for 5-6 minutes until the vegetables are tender-crisp.
4. In a small bowl, whisk together soy sauce, rice vinegar, and honey or maple syrup (if using).
5. Pour the sauce over the vegetables in the skillet and stir to combine, allowing the sauce to coat the vegetables evenly.
6. Add cooked brown rice to the skillet and stir-fry for an additional 2-3 minutes to heat through.
7. Taste and adjust seasoning if necessary, adding more soy sauce or salt as needed.
8. Remove from heat and transfer the vegetable stir-fry to serving plates.
9. Garnish with sesame seeds and sliced green onions, if desired.
10. Serve hot and enjoy this delicious and nutritious vegetable stir-fry with brown rice!

Nutritional Values (per serving):

- Calories: 320
- Fat: 8g
- Carbohydrates: 54g
- Protein: 10g

Lentil Soup with Whole Grain Rolls

Ingredients:

For the Lentil Soup:

- 1 cup dried green or brown lentils, rinsed and drained
- 1 tablespoon olive oil
- 1 onion, diced
- 2 carrots, diced
- 2 celery stalks, diced
- 3 cloves garlic, minced
- 1 teaspoon ground cumin
- 1 teaspoon ground coriander
- 1/2 teaspoon smoked paprika
- 1/4 teaspoon cayenne pepper (optional)
- 6 cups vegetable broth
- 1 can (14 oz) diced tomatoes
- Salt and pepper to taste
- Fresh parsley or cilantro for garnish (optional)

For the Whole Grain Rolls:

- 4 whole grain rolls
- Butter or olive oil for brushing (optional)

Directions:

For the Lentil Soup:

1. Heat olive oil in a large pot over medium heat. Add diced onion, carrots, and celery, and sauté for 5-6 minutes until softened.
2. Add minced garlic, ground cumin, ground coriander, smoked paprika, and cayenne pepper (if using) to the pot. Stir and cook for another 1-2 minutes until fragrant.
3. Add rinsed lentils, vegetable broth, and diced tomatoes to the pot. Bring to a boil, then reduce heat to low and let simmer, covered, for 25-30 minutes or until the lentils are tender.
4. Season with salt and pepper to taste.
5. Ladle the lentil soup into bowls, garnish with fresh parsley or cilantro if desired, and serve hot.

For the Whole Grain Rolls:

1. Preheat the oven to 350°F (175°C).
2. Place whole grain rolls on a baking sheet lined with parchment paper.
3. If desired, brush the tops of the rolls with melted butter or olive oil for a golden crust.
4. Bake in the preheated oven for 10-12 minutes, or until the rolls are warmed through and slightly crispy on the outside.
5. Remove from the oven and serve alongside the lentil soup.

Nutritional Values (per serving, including one roll):

- Calories: 350
- Fat: 7g
- Carbohydrates: 60g
- Protein: 15g

Tuna Salad Stuffed Bell Peppers

Ingredients:

- 4 large bell peppers (any color), halved and seeds removed
- 2 cans (5 oz each) tuna in water, drained
- 1/4 cup Greek yogurt or mayonnaise
- 1 tablespoon Dijon mustard
- 1/4 cup diced red onion
- 1/4 cup diced celery
- 1/4 cup diced cucumber
- 1/4 cup diced pickles
- 1 tablespoon lemon juice
- Salt and pepper to taste
- Fresh parsley or dill for garnish (optional)

Directions:

1. Preheat the oven to 375°F (190°C).
2. Place the bell pepper halves in a baking dish, cut side up.
3. In a large mixing bowl, combine the drained tuna, Greek yogurt or mayonnaise, Dijon mustard, diced red onion, diced celery, diced cucumber, diced pickles, and lemon juice. Mix well to combine.
4. Season the tuna salad mixture with salt and pepper to taste.
5. Spoon the tuna salad mixture evenly into each bell pepper half, pressing down gently to fill.
6. Cover the baking dish with aluminum foil and bake in the preheated oven for 20-25 minutes, or until the bell peppers are tender.
7. Remove the foil and bake for an additional 5 minutes to lightly brown the tops.
8. Remove from the oven and let cool slightly before serving.
9. Garnish with fresh parsley or dill, if desired.
10. Serve warm or at room temperature as a delicious and satisfying lunch option.

Nutritional Values (per serving, based on one stuffed bell pepper half):

- Calories: 150
- Fat: 3g
- Carbohydrates: 10g
- Protein: 20g

Grilled Salmon with Quinoa and Steamed Broccoli

Ingredients:

For the Grilled Salmon:

- 4 salmon fillets (6 oz each), skin-on or skinless
- 2 tablespoons olive oil
- 2 cloves garlic, minced
- 1 teaspoon lemon zest
- 1 tablespoon lemon juice
- Salt and pepper to taste

For the Quinoa:

- 1 cup quinoa, rinsed
- 2 cups water or vegetable broth
- Salt to taste

For the Steamed Broccoli:

- 2 heads broccoli, cut into florets
- Water for steaming
- Salt to taste

Directions:

For the Grilled Salmon:

1. Preheat the grill to medium-high heat.
2. In a small bowl, whisk together olive oil, minced garlic, lemon zest, lemon juice, salt, and pepper.
3. Brush the marinade over the salmon fillets, coating them evenly.
4. Place the salmon fillets on the grill, skin-side down if applicable.
5. Grill for 4-5 minutes per side, or until the salmon is cooked through and easily flakes with a fork.
6. Remove from the grill and set aside.

For the Quinoa:

1. In a medium saucepan, combine quinoa and water or vegetable broth.
2. Bring to a boil over medium-high heat, then reduce heat to low, cover, and simmer for 15-20 minutes, or until the quinoa is tender and the liquid is absorbed.
3. Fluff the cooked quinoa with a fork and season with salt to taste.

For the Steamed Broccoli:

1. Place broccoli florets in a steamer basket set over a pot of boiling water.
2. Cover and steam for 5-7 minutes, or until the broccoli is tender but still vibrant green.
3. Remove from the steamer basket and season with salt to taste.

Assembling the Meal:

1. Divide the cooked quinoa evenly among serving plates.
2. Top each serving of quinoa with a grilled salmon fillet.
3. Serve alongside steamed broccoli.
4. Optionally, garnish with lemon slices and fresh herbs like parsley or dill.
5. Serve hot and enjoy this nutritious and flavorful grilled salmon with quinoa and steamed broccoli!

Nutritional Values (per serving, including 1 salmon fillet, 1/4 of the quinoa, and 1/4 of the broccoli):

- Calories: 400
- Fat: 18g
- Carbohydrates: 26g
- Protein: 35g

DINNER

Day 1 to 7: Satisfying Evening Dinners

Baked Cod with Sweet Potato Fries

Ingredients:

For the Baked Cod:

- 4 cod fillets (6 oz each)
- 2 tablespoons olive oil
- 2 cloves garlic, minced
- 1 tablespoon lemon juice
- 1 teaspoon lemon zest
- 1 teaspoon paprika
- Salt and pepper to taste
- Fresh parsley for garnish (optional)

For the Sweet Potato Fries:

- 2 large sweet potatoes, peeled and cut into fries
- 2 tablespoons olive oil
- 1 teaspoon garlic powder
- 1 teaspoon paprika
- Salt and pepper to taste

Directions:

For the Baked Cod:

1. Preheat the oven to 400°F (200°C).
2. In a small bowl, mix together olive oil, minced garlic, lemon juice, lemon zest, paprika, salt, and pepper.
3. Place the cod fillets on a baking sheet lined with parchment paper or aluminum foil.
4. Brush the cod fillets with the prepared marinade, coating them evenly.
5. Bake in the preheated oven for 12-15 minutes, or until the cod is opaque and flakes easily with a fork.
6. Remove from the oven and garnish with fresh parsley, if desired.

For the Sweet Potato Fries:

1. Preheat the oven to 425°F (220°C).
2. In a large bowl, toss sweet potato fries with olive oil, garlic powder, paprika, salt, and pepper until evenly coated.
3. Spread the sweet potato fries in a single layer on a baking sheet lined with parchment paper.
4. Bake in the preheated oven for 20-25 minutes, flipping halfway through, until the fries are golden brown and crispy.

5. Remove from the oven and season with additional salt and pepper if desired.

Assembling the Meal:

1. Serve the baked cod fillets alongside the sweet potato fries.
2. Optionally, garnish the cod with fresh parsley and serve with lemon wedges for squeezing over the fish.
3. Enjoy this delicious and nutritious meal!

Nutritional Values (per serving, including 1 cod fillet and 1/4 of the sweet potato fries):

- Calories: 400
- Fat: 15g
- Carbohydrates: 35g
- Protein: 30g

Chicken and Mushroom Risotto

Ingredients:

- 1 cup Arborio rice
- 2 tablespoons olive oil
- 1 onion, finely chopped
- 2 cloves garlic, minced
- 8 oz chicken breast, diced
- 8 oz mushrooms (such as cremini or button), sliced
- 4 cups chicken or vegetable broth, warmed
- 1/2 cup dry white wine (optional)
- 1/2 cup grated Parmesan cheese
- 2 tablespoons unsalted butter
- Salt and pepper to taste
- Fresh parsley for garnish (optional)

Directions:

1. In a large skillet or saucepan, heat the olive oil over medium heat. Add the diced chicken breast and cook until browned and cooked through, about 5-7 minutes. Remove the chicken from the pan and set aside.
2. In the same skillet, add a bit more olive oil if needed, then add the chopped onion and minced garlic. Cook until the onion is soft and translucent, about 3-4 minutes.
3. Add the sliced mushrooms to the skillet and cook until they are golden brown and tender, about 5 minutes.
4. Return the cooked chicken to the skillet, along with the Arborio rice. Stir to combine and coat the rice with the oil and juices from the chicken and mushrooms.
5. If using, pour in the white wine and cook until it has mostly evaporated, stirring frequently.
6. Begin adding the warm chicken or vegetable broth to the skillet, one ladleful at a time, stirring frequently and allowing the rice to absorb the liquid before adding more. Continue this process until the rice is creamy and tender, about 18-20 minutes. You may not need all of the broth.
7. Once the rice is cooked to your desired consistency, stir in the grated Parmesan cheese and unsalted butter until melted and well combined. Season with salt and pepper to taste.
8. Remove the skillet from the heat and let the risotto rest for a few minutes to allow the flavors to meld together.
9. Serve the chicken and mushroom risotto hot, garnished with fresh parsley if desired.

Nutritional Values (per serving):

- Calories: 380
- Fat: 14g
- Carbohydrates: 40g
- Protein: 22g

Beef Stir-Fry with Vegetables and Tamari Sauce

Ingredients:

- 1 lb beef steak (flank steak or sirloin), thinly sliced against the grain
- 2 tablespoons tamari sauce (or soy sauce)
- 2 tablespoons rice vinegar
- 2 tablespoons honey or maple syrup
- 2 cloves garlic, minced
- 1 teaspoon fresh ginger, grated
- 2 tablespoons vegetable oil, divided
- 1 onion, sliced
- 2 bell peppers (red, yellow, or green), sliced
- 1 cup broccoli florets
- 1 cup snap peas
- Cooked rice or noodles, for serving
- Sesame seeds and chopped green onions, for garnish (optional)

Directions:

1. In a small bowl, whisk together the tamari sauce, rice vinegar, honey or maple syrup, minced garlic, and grated ginger to make the marinade.
2. Place the thinly sliced beef in a shallow dish or resealable plastic bag. Pour half of the marinade over the beef, reserving the remaining marinade for later. Toss the beef to coat evenly in the marinade. Let it marinate in the refrigerator for at least 30 minutes, or up to 2 hours.
3. Heat 1 tablespoon of vegetable oil in a large skillet or wok over medium-high heat. Once hot, add the marinated beef slices in a single layer, working in batches if necessary to avoid overcrowding the pan. Cook for 2-3 minutes per side, or until the beef is browned and cooked to your desired level of doneness. Remove the cooked beef from the skillet and set aside.
4. In the same skillet, add the remaining tablespoon of vegetable oil. Add the sliced onion, bell peppers, broccoli florets, and snap peas. Stir-fry for 4-5 minutes, or until the vegetables are crisp-tender.
5. Return the cooked beef to the skillet with the vegetables. Pour the reserved marinade over the beef and vegetables. Stir well to combine and coat everything in the sauce. Cook for an additional 1-2 minutes, or until the sauce has thickened slightly.
6. Remove the skillet from the heat. Serve the beef stir-fry hot over cooked rice or noodles. Garnish with sesame seeds and chopped green onions, if desired.

Nutritional Values (per serving, excluding rice or noodles):

- Calories: 320
- Fat: 18g
- Carbohydrates: 16g
- Protein: 25g

Vegetarian Chili with Cornbread

Ingredients:

For the Vegetarian Chili:

- 1 tablespoon olive oil
- 1 onion, diced
- 2 cloves garlic, minced
- 1 bell pepper, diced (any color)
- 1 carrot, diced
- 1 zucchini, diced
- 1 cup corn kernels (fresh or frozen)
- 1 can (15 oz) black beans, drained and rinsed
- 1 can (15 oz) kidney beans, drained and rinsed
- 1 can (15 oz) diced tomatoes
- 1 can (6 oz) tomato paste
- 2 cups vegetable broth
- 2 teaspoons chili powder
- 1 teaspoon ground cumin
- 1 teaspoon smoked paprika
- Salt and pepper to taste
- Optional toppings: shredded cheese, sour cream, sliced green onions, chopped cilantro

For the Cornbread:

- 1 cup cornmeal
- 1 cup all-purpose flour
- 1/4 cup granulated sugar
- 1 tablespoon baking powder
- 1/2 teaspoon salt
- 1 cup milk (or dairy-free alternative)
- 1/4 cup vegetable oil
- 1 egg (or flax egg for vegan option)

Directions:

For the Vegetarian Chili:

1. Heat olive oil in a large pot or Dutch oven over medium heat. Add diced onion and cook until translucent, about 3-4 minutes.
2. Add minced garlic and diced bell pepper, carrot, and zucchini to the pot. Cook for another 5 minutes, stirring occasionally, until the vegetables are softened.
3. Stir in corn kernels, black beans, kidney beans, diced tomatoes, tomato paste, vegetable broth, chili powder, cumin, smoked paprika, salt, and pepper.
4. Bring the chili to a simmer, then reduce the heat to low. Cover and let it simmer for 20-25 minutes, stirring occasionally, to allow the flavors to meld together and the chili to thicken.

For the Cornbread:

1. Preheat the oven to 400°F (200°C). Grease a 9x9-inch baking dish or line it with parchment paper.
2. In a large mixing bowl, whisk together cornmeal, all-purpose flour, sugar, baking powder, and salt.
3. In a separate bowl, whisk together milk, vegetable oil, and egg until well combined.
4. Pour the wet ingredients into the dry ingredients and stir until just combined. Be careful not to overmix; a few lumps are okay.
5. Pour the cornbread batter into the prepared baking dish and spread it evenly.
6. Bake in the preheated oven for 20-25 minutes, or until the cornbread is golden brown on top and a toothpick inserted into the center comes out clean.

7. Remove the cornbread from the oven and let it cool slightly before slicing.

Assembling the Meal:

1. Ladle the warm vegetarian chili into bowls.
2. Serve slices of cornbread alongside the chili.
3. Optionally, top the chili with shredded cheese, sour cream, sliced green onions, or chopped cilantro.

Nutritional Values (per serving, excluding optional toppings):

- Calories: 380
- Fat: 12g
- Carbohydrates: 58g
- Protein: 13g

Pork Tenderloin with Apple Sauce and Green Beans

Ingredients:

For the Pork Tenderloin:

- 1 lb pork tenderloin
- 1 tablespoon olive oil
- 2 cloves garlic, minced
- 1 teaspoon dried thyme
- Salt and pepper to taste

For the Apple Sauce:

- 2 apples, peeled, cored, and diced (use sweet varieties like Fuji or Gala)
- 1 tablespoon unsalted butter
- 1 tablespoon brown sugar (optional)
- 1/4 teaspoon ground cinnamon
- Pinch of salt

For the Green Beans:

- 1 lb green beans, trimmed
- 1 tablespoon olive oil
- 2 cloves garlic, minced
- Salt and pepper to taste

Directions:

For the Pork Tenderloin:

1. Preheat the oven to 400°F (200°C).
2. In a small bowl, combine minced garlic, dried thyme, salt, and pepper.
3. Rub the pork tenderloin all over with the olive oil, then rub the garlic and thyme mixture onto the pork, ensuring it's evenly coated.
4. Place the seasoned pork tenderloin on a baking sheet lined with parchment paper or aluminum foil.
5. Roast in the preheated oven for 25-30 minutes, or until the internal temperature reaches 145°F (63°C) for medium doneness. Remove from the oven and let it rest for a few minutes before slicing.

For the Apple Sauce:

1. While the pork is roasting, prepare the apple sauce. In a saucepan, melt the unsalted butter over medium heat.
2. Add the diced apples to the saucepan, along with the brown sugar (if using), ground cinnamon, and a pinch of salt.
3. Cook the apples, stirring occasionally, until they are soft and tender, about 8-10 minutes.
4. Once the apples are cooked, remove the saucepan from the heat and mash the apples with a fork or potato masher until you reach your desired consistency. Keep warm until ready to serve.

For the Green Beans:

1. In a large skillet, heat olive oil over medium heat. Add minced garlic

and cook for about 1 minute, or until fragrant.

2. Add the trimmed green beans to the skillet and season with salt and pepper to taste. Cook, stirring occasionally, until the green beans are crisp-tender, about 5-7 minutes.

Assembling the Meal:

1. Slice the rested pork tenderloin into medallions.
2. Serve the pork tenderloin alongside the apple sauce and green beans.

Nutritional Values (per serving):

- Calories: 320
- Fat: 12g
- Carbohydrates: 20g
- Protein: 30g

Pasta Primavera with a Light Tomato Sauce

Ingredients:

For the Pasta Primavera:

- 8 oz (225g) pasta of your choice (penne, fusilli, or spaghetti)
- 2 tablespoons olive oil
- 2 cloves garlic, minced
- 1 onion, thinly sliced
- 1 bell pepper, thinly sliced
- 1 zucchini, thinly sliced
- 1 cup cherry tomatoes, halved
- 1 cup broccoli florets
- 1 cup sliced mushrooms
- Salt and pepper to taste
- Grated Parmesan cheese, for serving (optional)
- Chopped fresh parsley, for garnish (optional)

For the Light Tomato Sauce:

- 1 tablespoon olive oil
- 2 cloves garlic, minced
- 1 can (14 oz) diced tomatoes
- 1 teaspoon dried Italian herbs (basil, oregano, thyme)
- Salt and pepper to taste

Directions:

1. Cook the pasta according to the package instructions until al dente. Drain and set aside.
2. While the pasta is cooking, prepare the vegetables and sauce.
3. For the Light Tomato Sauce: In a saucepan, heat olive oil over medium heat. Add minced garlic and cook until fragrant, about 1 minute. Add the diced tomatoes (with their juices) and dried Italian herbs. Season with salt and pepper to taste. Simmer the sauce for 10-15 minutes, stirring occasionally, until slightly thickened.
4. For the Pasta Primavera: In a large skillet, heat olive oil over medium heat. Add minced garlic and thinly sliced onion. Cook until the onion is translucent, about 3-4 minutes.
5. Add thinly sliced bell pepper, zucchini, cherry tomatoes, broccoli florets, and sliced mushrooms to the skillet. Cook, stirring occasionally, for 5-7 minutes, or until the vegetables are tender-crisp.
6. Once the vegetables are cooked, add the cooked pasta to the skillet. Pour the light tomato sauce over the pasta and vegetables. Toss everything together until well combined. Season with salt and pepper to taste.
7. Remove the skillet from the heat. Serve the pasta primavera hot, garnished with grated Parmesan

cheese and chopped fresh parsley, if desired.

Nutritional Values (per serving, without optional toppings):

- Calories: 350
- Fat: 10g
- Carbohydrates: 55g
- Protein: 12g

Cauliflower Steak with Tahini Sauce

Ingredients:

For the Cauliflower Steak:

- 1 large head cauliflower
- 2 tablespoons olive oil
- 1 teaspoon smoked paprika
- 1/2 teaspoon garlic powder
- Salt and pepper to taste

For the Tahini Sauce:

- 1/4 cup tahini
- 2 tablespoons lemon juice
- 2 tablespoons water
- 1 clove garlic, minced
- 1/2 teaspoon ground cumin
- Salt to taste

Optional Garnish:

- Chopped fresh parsley
- Toasted sesame seeds

Directions:

1. Preheat the oven to 425°F (220°C). Line a baking sheet with parchment paper.
2. Remove the leaves from the cauliflower and trim the stem, leaving the core intact. Slice the cauliflower into 1-inch thick slices to create "steaks." You should get about 2-3 steaks from one head of cauliflower.
3. In a small bowl, whisk together olive oil, smoked paprika, garlic powder, salt, and pepper.
4. Brush both sides of each cauliflower steak with the seasoned olive oil mixture and place them on the prepared baking sheet.
5. Roast the cauliflower steaks in the preheated oven for 25-30 minutes, or until they are tender and golden brown, flipping halfway through the cooking time.
6. While the cauliflower is roasting, prepare the tahini sauce. In a small bowl, whisk together tahini, lemon juice, water, minced garlic, ground cumin, and salt until smooth and creamy. If the sauce is too thick, add more water, 1 tablespoon at a time, until desired consistency is reached.
7. Once the cauliflower steaks are done, transfer them to serving plates. Drizzle each steak with tahini sauce and sprinkle with chopped fresh parsley and toasted sesame seeds, if desired.
8. Serve the cauliflower steaks immediately with additional tahini sauce on the side, if desired.

Nutritional Values (per serving):

- Calories: 180
- Fat: 14g
- Carbohydrates: 11g
- Protein: 6g

SNACKS

Day 1 to 7: Quick and Healthy Options

Hummus with Carrot and Celery Sticks

Ingredients:

For the Hummus:

- 1 can (15 oz) chickpeas, drained and rinsed
- 2 tablespoons tahini
- 2 tablespoons lemon juice
- 1 clove garlic, minced
- 2 tablespoons olive oil
- 1/2 teaspoon ground cumin
- Salt to taste
- Water (as needed for desired consistency)

For Serving:
- Carrot sticks
- Celery sticks

Optional Garnish:
- Paprika
- Chopped fresh parsley
- Extra virgin olive oil

Directions:
1. In a food processor, combine the drained and rinsed chickpeas, tahini, lemon juice, minced garlic, olive oil, ground cumin, and a pinch of salt.
2. Blend the ingredients until smooth and creamy. If the hummus is too thick, gradually add water, 1 tablespoon at a time, until you reach your desired consistency.
3. Taste the hummus and adjust seasoning with more salt or lemon juice if needed.
4. Transfer the hummus to a serving bowl and garnish with a sprinkle of paprika, chopped fresh parsley, and a drizzle of extra virgin olive oil, if desired.
5. Serve the hummus alongside carrot and celery sticks for dipping.

Nutritional Values (per serving, without optional garnishes):
- Calories: 120
- Fat: 7g
- Carbohydrates: 11g
- Protein: 4g

Almonds and Dried Cranberries

Ingredients:
- Almonds
- Dried cranberries

Directions:
1. Measure out desired portions of almonds and dried cranberries.
2. Mix them together in a bowl or portion them into snack-sized containers.

Optional Variation:
- You can also add other nuts or dried fruits like walnuts, cashews, raisins, or apricots to create your own custom trail mix.

Nutritional Values (per serving):
- Almonds:
  - Calories: 160 (per 1 oz serving)
  - Fat: 14g
  - Carbohydrates: 6g
  - Protein: 6g
- Dried Cranberries:
  - Calories: 130 (per 1/4 cup serving)
  - Fat: 0g
  - Carbohydrates: 33g
  - Protein: 0g

Greek Yogurt with Honey and Almonds

Ingredients:
- Greek yogurt
- Honey
- Almonds, sliced or chopped

Directions:

1. Spoon desired amount of Greek yogurt into a serving bowl.
2. Drizzle honey over the Greek yogurt according to taste.
3. Sprinkle sliced or chopped almonds on top of the yogurt.
4. Serve immediately.

Optional Variation:

- You can add additional toppings such as fresh berries, granola, or cinnamon for extra flavor and texture.

Nutritional Values (per serving):

- Greek Yogurt:
  - Calories: 100-150 (depending on serving size)
  - Fat: 0-5g
  - Carbohydrates: 6-10g
  - Protein: 10-20g
- Honey (1 tablespoon):
  - Calories: 60
  - Fat: 0g
  - Carbohydrates: 17g
  - Protein: 0g
- Almonds (1 oz):
  - Calories: 160
  - Fat: 14g
  - Carbohydrates: 6g
  - Protein: 6g

Fresh Fruit Salad

Ingredients:

- Assorted fresh fruits (e.g., strawberries, blueberries, pineapple, grapes, kiwi, oranges, apples, etc.)

Optional Additions:

- Fresh mint leaves, finely chopped
- Honey or maple syrup (for a touch of sweetness)
- Lemon or lime juice (to prevent fruit from browning)

Directions:

1. Wash and prepare the fruits by removing any stems, cores, seeds, or peels as needed.
2. Cut the fruits into bite-sized pieces and place them in a large mixing bowl.
3. Gently toss the fruits together until well combined.
4. If desired, add a drizzle of honey or maple syrup for extra sweetness, and a squeeze of lemon or lime juice to enhance the flavors.
5. Garnish the fruit salad with finely chopped mint leaves for a refreshing touch.
6. Serve the fresh fruit salad immediately, or refrigerate it for up to a few hours before serving to allow the flavors to meld together.

Nutritional Values (per serving):

- Nutritional values will vary depending on the types and amounts of fruits used in the salad.

Cucumber Slices with Cream Cheese

Ingredients:

- Cucumber, washed and sliced into rounds
- Cream cheese, softened
- Optional: Everything bagel seasoning, dill, or chives for garnish

Directions:

1. Slice the cucumber into rounds, approximately ¼ inch thick.
2. Spread a dollop of softened cream cheese onto each cucumber slice.

3. Optionally, sprinkle with everything bagel seasoning, dill, or chives for added flavor and garnish.
4. Arrange the cucumber slices with cream cheese on a serving platter.

Optional Variation:

- You can also add smoked salmon or sliced turkey on top of the cream cheese for extra protein and flavor.

Nutritional Values (per serving, approximate):

- Calories: 50-70 (depending on serving size and amount of cream cheese)
- Fat: 4-6g
- Carbohydrates: 2-3g
- Protein: 1-2g

Rice Cakes with Peanut Butter and Banana

Ingredients:

- Rice cakes (choose your preferred variety)
- Peanut butter (smooth or crunchy)
- Ripe banana, sliced

Directions:

1. Spread a generous layer of peanut butter onto each rice cake.
2. Arrange banana slices on top of the peanut butter layer.
3. Serve immediately and enjoy!

Optional Variations:

- Drizzle honey or maple syrup over the banana slices for added sweetness.
- Sprinkle cinnamon or cocoa powder over the peanut butter for extra flavor.
- Add a sprinkle of chia seeds or crushed nuts for added texture and nutrition.

Nutritional Values (per serving, approximate):

- Calories: 150-200 (depending on serving size and amount of peanut butter)
- Fat: 8-12g
- Carbohydrates: 15-20g
- Protein: 4-6g

Air-Popped Popcorn with a Sprinkle of Nutritional Yeast

Ingredients:

- Popcorn kernels
- Nutritional yeast
- Optional: Salt to taste

Directions:

1. Prepare the popcorn using an air popper according to the manufacturer's instructions. If you don't have an air popper, you can also pop the kernels in a covered pot on the stovetop with a little bit of oil.
2. Once the popcorn is popped, transfer it to a large bowl.
3. Sprinkle nutritional yeast over the popcorn while it's still warm. Toss gently to coat evenly.
4. If desired, add a pinch of salt to taste.
5. Serve immediately and enjoy!

Optional Variation:

- You can add other seasonings such as garlic powder, onion powder, or smoked paprika for additional flavor.

Nutritional Values (per serving, approximate):

- Calories: 30-50 (depending on serving size)
- Fat: 0-2g
- Carbohydrates: 5-10g
- Protein: 1-2g

SCAN THE QR CODE AND IMMEDIATELY ACCESS YOUR 3 SPECIAL BONUSES IN DIGITAL FORMAT!

🔥 **Bonus 1: Dining Out Without Derailing Your Diet**

🔥 **Bonus 2: Recognizing Your Body Type**

🔥 **Bonus 3: Weekly Grocery Planner**

WEEK 2

INTENSIFYING VARIETY AND FLAVOR

BREAKFAST

Day 8 to 14: Flavorful Morning Boosts

Chia Seed Pudding with Coconut Milk and Mango

Ingredients:

- 1/4 cup chia seeds
- 1 cup coconut milk (can use canned coconut milk or coconut beverage)
- 1 ripe mango, diced
- Optional: Sweetener of choice (e.g., honey, maple syrup, agave nectar), to taste
- Optional toppings: Sliced almonds, shredded coconut, additional diced mango

Directions:

1. In a mixing bowl, combine the chia seeds and coconut milk. Stir well to ensure the chia seeds are evenly distributed and not clumping together.
2. If desired, sweeten the mixture with your choice of sweetener to taste.
3. Cover the bowl and refrigerate the chia seed mixture for at least 4 hours or overnight, allowing the chia seeds to absorb the liquid and form a pudding-like consistency.
4. Once the chia seed pudding has set, give it a good stir to break up any clumps and ensure a smooth texture.
5. To serve, divide the chia seed pudding into individual bowls or jars. Top each serving with diced mango and any optional toppings of your choice.
6. Enjoy this delicious and nutritious chia seed pudding with coconut milk and mango for a flavorful morning boost!

Nutritional Values (per serving, approximate):

- Calories: 200-250 (depending on serving size and sweetener used)
- Fat: 12-15g
- Carbohydrates: 20-25g
- Protein: 5-7g

Oatmeal with Apples and Cinnamon

Ingredients:

- 1/2 cup rolled oats
- 1 cup water or milk of choice (e.g., cow's milk, almond milk, soy milk)
- 1 small apple, diced
- 1/2 teaspoon ground cinnamon
- Optional toppings: Sliced almonds, raisins, maple syrup, honey

Directions:

1. In a small saucepan, combine the rolled oats and water or milk. Bring to a boil over medium heat.
2. Once boiling, reduce the heat to low and simmer, stirring occasionally, for about 5 minutes or until the oats are cooked to your desired consistency.
3. While the oats are cooking, prepare the diced apple. You can peel the apple first if desired, but leaving

the peel on adds extra fiber and nutrients.
4. Add the diced apple to the saucepan with the cooking oats. Stir in the ground cinnamon.
5. Continue to cook the oatmeal with the apples and cinnamon for an additional 2-3 minutes, or until the apples are softened and the oatmeal is heated through.
6. Once cooked, remove the oatmeal from the heat and transfer it to serving bowls.
7. Serve the oatmeal hot, optionally garnished with additional toppings such as sliced almonds, raisins, maple syrup, or honey.

Nutritional Values (per serving, approximate):

- Calories: 250-300 (depending on type of milk and toppings)
- Fat: 4-6g
- Carbohydrates: 45-50g
- Protein: 6-8g

Protein-Packed Smoothie with Spinach, Blueberry, and Avocado

Ingredients:

- 1 cup fresh spinach leaves
- 1/2 cup frozen blueberries
- 1/2 ripe avocado, peeled and pitted
- 1 scoop protein powder (vanilla or unflavored)
- 1 cup milk of choice (e.g., almond milk, soy milk, cow's milk)
- Optional: Sweetener of choice (e.g., honey, maple syrup, agave nectar) to taste
- Ice cubes (optional, for a colder smoothie)

Directions:

1. In a blender, combine the fresh spinach leaves, frozen blueberries, ripe avocado, protein powder, and milk of choice.
2. If desired, add a sweetener of your choice to taste. This step is optional, as the sweetness from the blueberries and protein powder may be sufficient.
3. Optional: Add ice cubes to the blender for a colder and thicker smoothie.
4. Blend on high speed until smooth and creamy, ensuring all ingredients are well combined.
5. If the smoothie is too thick, you can add more milk to reach your desired consistency.
6. Once blended to your liking, pour the smoothie into glasses and serve immediately.

Nutritional Values (per serving, approximate):

- Calories: 250-300 (depending on type of milk and protein powder)
- Fat: 15-20g
- Carbohydrates: 20-25g
- Protein: 15-20g

Egg Muffins with Kale, Mushrooms, and Red Peppers

Ingredients:

- 6 large eggs
- 1 cup kale, chopped
- 1/2 cup mushrooms, sliced
- 1/2 cup red bell peppers, diced
- Salt and pepper, to taste
- Cooking spray or olive oil for greasing muffin tin

Directions:

1. Preheat your oven to 350°F (175°C). Grease a muffin tin with cooking spray or olive oil to prevent sticking.
2. In a mixing bowl, crack the eggs and whisk them together until well beaten.
3. Add the chopped kale, sliced mushrooms, and diced red bell peppers to the bowl with the beaten eggs. Season with salt and pepper to taste.
4. Stir the ingredients until they are evenly distributed in the egg mixture.
5. Pour the egg and vegetable mixture evenly into the prepared muffin tin, filling each muffin cup about 3/4 full.
6. Place the muffin tin in the preheated oven and bake for 20-25 minutes, or until the egg muffins are set and slightly golden on top.
7. Once cooked, remove the muffin tin from the oven and allow the egg muffins to cool for a few minutes before removing them from the tin.
8. Use a butter knife to gently loosen the edges of the egg muffins from the muffin tin, then transfer them to a wire rack to cool completely.
9. Serve the egg muffins warm or at room temperature. Enjoy as a nutritious breakfast or snack!

Nutritional Values (per serving, approximate, based on 1 egg muffin):

- Calories: 70-90
- Fat: 4-6g
- Carbohydrates: 2-4g
- Protein: 6-8g

Almond Butter and Banana Toast on Sprouted Grain Bread

Ingredients:

- 2 slices of sprouted grain bread
- 2 tablespoons almond butter
- 1 ripe banana, thinly sliced
- Optional toppings: Drizzle of honey, sprinkle of cinnamon

Directions:

1. Toast the sprouted grain bread slices until they are golden brown and crispy.
2. Once toasted, spread a tablespoon of almond butter evenly onto each slice of toast.
3. Arrange the thinly sliced banana on top of the almond butter-covered toast slices.
4. If desired, drizzle a little honey over the banana slices and sprinkle with cinnamon for extra flavor.
5. Serve immediately and enjoy this delicious and nutritious almond butter and banana toast!

Nutritional Values (per serving, approximate):

- Calories: 300-350 (depending on bread and almond butter)
- Fat: 15-20g
- Carbohydrates: 35-45g
- Protein: 8-10g

Cottage Cheese with Sliced Peaches

Ingredients:

- 1/2 cup cottage cheese
- 1 ripe peach, sliced
- Optional: Drizzle of honey or sprinkle of cinnamon (optional)

Directions:

1. Place the cottage cheese in a serving bowl or onto a plate.
2. Wash and slice the ripe peach into thin slices.
3. Arrange the sliced peaches on top of the cottage cheese.
4. Optional: Drizzle a little honey over the cottage cheese and peaches for added sweetness, or sprinkle with cinnamon for extra flavor.
5. Serve immediately and enjoy this simple and delicious cottage cheese with sliced peaches!

Nutritional Values (per serving, approximate):

- Calories: 120-150 (depending on size of peach and amount of cottage cheese)
- Fat: 2-4g
- Carbohydrates: 15-20g
- Protein: 10-12g

Savory Breakfast Quinoa with Eggs and Spinach

Ingredients:

- 1/2 cup quinoa, rinsed
- 1 cup water or vegetable broth
- 2 eggs
- 1 cup fresh spinach leaves
- 1 tablespoon olive oil
- Salt and pepper, to taste
- Optional toppings: Sliced avocado, chopped tomatoes, grated Parmesan cheese

Directions:

1. In a small saucepan, combine the quinoa and water or vegetable broth. Bring to a boil over medium heat, then reduce the heat to low, cover, and simmer for about 15 minutes, or until the quinoa is cooked and the liquid is absorbed.
2. While the quinoa is cooking, heat the olive oil in a skillet over medium heat. Add the fresh spinach leaves and sauté until wilted, about 2-3 minutes. Season with salt and pepper to taste.
3. Push the wilted spinach to one side of the skillet and crack the eggs into the empty space. Cook the eggs to your desired level of doneness (e.g., scrambled, sunny-side-up, over easy).
4. Once the quinoa is cooked, fluff it with a fork and divide it between two serving bowls.
5. Top the quinoa with the sautéed spinach and cooked eggs.
6. If desired, garnish with sliced avocado, chopped tomatoes, or grated Parmesan cheese.
7. Serve immediately and enjoy this savory breakfast quinoa with eggs and spinach!

Nutritional Values (per serving, approximate):

- Calories: 350-400 (depending on toppings and portion sizes)
- Fat: 15-20g
- Carbohydrates: 30-35g
- Protein: 20-25g

LUNCH

Day 8 to 14: Diverse Midday Delights

Chicken Caesar Salad with Greek Yogurt Dressing

Ingredients:

- 2 boneless, skinless chicken breasts

- 1 tablespoon olive oil
- Salt and pepper, to taste
- 1 head romaine lettuce, washed and chopped
- 1/4 cup grated Parmesan cheese
- 1/4 cup croutons
- Lemon wedges (for garnish)

For the Greek Yogurt Dressing:

- 1/2 cup plain Greek yogurt
- 2 tablespoons lemon juice
- 1 tablespoon Dijon mustard
- 1 clove garlic, minced
- 1 tablespoon grated Parmesan cheese
- Salt and pepper, to taste

Directions:

1. Preheat your grill or grill pan over medium-high heat. Season the chicken breasts with olive oil, salt, and pepper.
2. Grill the chicken breasts for about 6-7 minutes per side, or until cooked through and no longer pink in the center. Remove from the grill and let them rest for a few minutes before slicing.
3. While the chicken is cooking, prepare the Greek yogurt dressing. In a small bowl, whisk together the Greek yogurt, lemon juice, Dijon mustard, minced garlic, grated Parmesan cheese, salt, and pepper until smooth and well combined. Adjust seasoning to taste.
4. Once the chicken has rested, slice it into thin strips.
5. In a large salad bowl, combine the chopped romaine lettuce, sliced chicken breast, grated Parmesan cheese, and croutons.
6. Drizzle the Greek yogurt dressing over the salad and toss gently to coat all the ingredients evenly.
7. Divide the salad among plates, garnish with lemon wedges, and serve immediately.

Nutritional Values (per serving, approximate):

- Calories: 350-400
- Fat: 15-20g
- Carbohydrates: 15-20g
- Protein: 30-35g

Sweet Potato and Black Bean Burrito

Ingredients:

- 2 large sweet potatoes, peeled and diced into small cubes
- 1 can (15 ounces) black beans, drained and rinsed
- 1 bell pepper, diced
- 1 onion, diced
- 2 cloves garlic, minced
- 1 teaspoon ground cumin
- 1 teaspoon chili powder
- Salt and pepper, to taste
- 4 large whole wheat or flour tortillas
- 1 cup shredded cheese (cheddar, Monterey Jack, or Mexican blend)
- Optional toppings: Salsa, avocado slices, Greek yogurt or sour cream, chopped cilantro

Directions:

1. Heat a tablespoon of olive oil in a large skillet over medium heat. Add the diced sweet potatoes and cook for about 10-12 minutes, or until they are tender and lightly browned.
2. Add the diced bell pepper and onion to the skillet with the sweet

potatoes. Cook for an additional 5 minutes, until the vegetables are softened.
3. Stir in the minced garlic, ground cumin, and chili powder. Cook for another minute until the spices are fragrant. Season with salt and pepper to taste.
4. Add the drained black beans to the skillet and stir to combine. Cook for another 2-3 minutes, until the beans are heated through.
5. Warm the tortillas in a dry skillet or microwave for a few seconds to make them pliable.
6. Divide the sweet potato and black bean mixture evenly among the tortillas. Sprinkle shredded cheese over the filling.
7. Roll up the tortillas tightly, folding in the sides as you go, to form burritos.
8. Optional: Heat a clean skillet over medium heat and place the burritos seam-side down. Cook for 2-3 minutes on each side until golden and crispy.
9. Serve the burritos warm with your favorite toppings such as salsa, avocado slices, Greek yogurt or sour cream, and chopped cilantro.

Nutritional Values (per serving, approximate):

- Calories: 400-450
- Fat: 10-15g
- Carbohydrates: 60-70g
- Protein: 15-20g

Grilled Shrimp with Mango Salsa

Ingredients:

- 1 pound large shrimp, peeled and deveined
- 2 tablespoons olive oil
- 1 teaspoon smoked paprika
- 1/2 teaspoon garlic powder
- Salt and pepper, to taste
- 2 ripe mangoes, peeled, pitted, and diced
- 1/2 red onion, finely chopped
- 1 red bell pepper, diced
- 1 jalapeño pepper, seeded and minced
- 1/4 cup fresh cilantro, chopped
- Juice of 1 lime
- Salt and pepper, to taste

Directions:

1. Preheat your grill or grill pan to medium-high heat.
2. In a bowl, toss the shrimp with olive oil, smoked paprika, garlic powder, salt, and pepper until evenly coated.
3. Thread the seasoned shrimp onto skewers.
4. Grill the shrimp skewers for 2-3 minutes per side, or until they are opaque and cooked through. Remove from the grill and set aside.
5. In a separate bowl, combine the diced mangoes, red onion, red bell pepper, jalapeño pepper, cilantro, lime juice, salt, and pepper to make the mango salsa. Mix well.
6. Serve the grilled shrimp skewers with the mango salsa on the side.

Nutritional Values (per serving, approximate):

- Calories: 250-300
- Fat: 10-15g
- Carbohydrates: 20-25g

- Protein: 20-25g

Turkey Meatballs with Spaghetti Squash

Ingredients:

- 1 spaghetti squash
- 1 pound ground turkey
- 1/4 cup breadcrumbs
- 1/4 cup grated Parmesan cheese
- 1 egg, lightly beaten
- 2 cloves garlic, minced
- 1 teaspoon dried oregano
- 1 teaspoon dried basil
- 1/2 teaspoon salt
- 1/4 teaspoon black pepper
- Olive oil, for drizzling
- Fresh parsley, chopped (for garnish)
- Marinara sauce (optional, for serving)

Directions:

1. Preheat your oven to 400°F (200°C).
2. Cut the spaghetti squash in half lengthwise and scoop out the seeds. Place the squash halves, cut side down, on a baking sheet lined with parchment paper.
3. Bake the spaghetti squash in the preheated oven for 40-45 minutes, or until the flesh is tender and easily pierced with a fork. Remove from the oven and let it cool slightly.
4. While the squash is baking, prepare the turkey meatballs. In a large mixing bowl, combine the ground turkey, breadcrumbs, grated Parmesan cheese, beaten egg, minced garlic, dried oregano, dried basil, salt, and black pepper. Mix until well combined.
5. Shape the turkey mixture into meatballs, using about 1 tablespoon of mixture for each meatball.
6. Heat a drizzle of olive oil in a large skillet over medium heat. Add the meatballs to the skillet and cook for 6-8 minutes, turning occasionally, until browned on all sides and cooked through.
7. While the meatballs are cooking, use a fork to scrape the flesh of the baked spaghetti squash into strands.
8. Serve the turkey meatballs over the spaghetti squash strands. Garnish with chopped parsley and serve with marinara sauce on the side if desired.

Nutritional Values (per serving, approximate):

- Calories: 300-350
- Fat: 15-20g
- Carbohydrates: 15-20g
- Protein: 25-30g

Stuffed Acorn Squash with Quinoa and Cranberries

Ingredients:

- 2 acorn squash, halved and seeds removed
- 1 cup quinoa, rinsed
- 2 cups vegetable broth or water
- 1 tablespoon olive oil
- 1 onion, diced
- 2 cloves garlic, minced
- 1 teaspoon dried thyme
- 1/2 teaspoon ground cinnamon
- 1/2 cup dried cranberries

- 1/4 cup chopped pecans or walnuts
- Salt and pepper, to taste
- Fresh parsley, chopped (for garnish)

Directions:

1. Preheat your oven to 400°F (200°C). Place the halved acorn squash, cut side down, on a baking sheet lined with parchment paper. Bake for 30-35 minutes, or until the squash is tender when pierced with a fork.
2. While the squash is baking, prepare the quinoa. In a medium saucepan, combine the quinoa and vegetable broth or water. Bring to a boil, then reduce the heat to low, cover, and simmer for 15-20 minutes, or until the quinoa is cooked and the liquid is absorbed.
3. In a large skillet, heat the olive oil over medium heat. Add the diced onion and cook for 5-6 minutes, until softened and translucent.
4. Add the minced garlic, dried thyme, and ground cinnamon to the skillet. Cook for an additional minute until fragrant.
5. Stir in the cooked quinoa, dried cranberries, and chopped nuts. Season with salt and pepper to taste. Cook for another 2-3 minutes to allow the flavors to blend.
6. Once the acorn squash halves are cooked, remove them from the oven. Carefully flip them over so the cut side is facing up.
7. Spoon the quinoa mixture into each acorn squash half, packing it down gently.
8. Return the stuffed squash to the oven and bake for another 10-15 minutes, or until heated through and lightly browned on top.
9. Garnish with chopped fresh parsley before serving.

Nutritional Values (per serving, approximate):

- Calories: 300-350
- Fat: 8-10g
- Carbohydrates: 50-60g
- Protein: 7-9g

Baked Tilapia with Lemon Herb Quinoa

Ingredients:

- 4 tilapia fillets
- 1 lemon, sliced
- Salt and pepper, to taste
- 1 cup quinoa, rinsed
- 2 cups vegetable broth or water
- 2 tablespoons fresh lemon juice
- 2 tablespoons chopped fresh parsley
- 1 tablespoon chopped fresh dill
- 1 tablespoon chopped fresh chives
- 2 tablespoons olive oil

Directions:

1. Preheat your oven to 375°F (190°C).
2. Season the tilapia fillets with salt and pepper on both sides, then place them in a baking dish.
3. Arrange lemon slices on top of the tilapia fillets.
4. Bake the tilapia in the preheated oven for 15-20 minutes, or until the fish is opaque and flakes easily with a fork.
5. While the tilapia is baking, prepare the lemon herb quinoa. In a

medium saucepan, combine the quinoa and vegetable broth or water. Bring to a boil, then reduce the heat to low, cover, and simmer for 15-20 minutes, or until the quinoa is cooked and the liquid is absorbed.

6. Fluff the cooked quinoa with a fork, then stir in the fresh lemon juice, chopped parsley, dill, chives, and olive oil. Season with salt and pepper to taste.
7. Serve the baked tilapia fillets alongside the lemon herb quinoa.

Nutritional Values (per serving, approximate):

- Calories: 250-300
- Fat: 7-9g
- Carbohydrates: 20-25g
- Protein: 25-30g

Vegetable and Goat Cheese Frittata

Ingredients:

- 8 large eggs
- 1/4 cup milk or cream
- 1 tablespoon olive oil
- 1 small onion, diced
- 1 bell pepper, diced
- 1 cup sliced mushrooms
- 2 cups fresh spinach leaves
- 1/4 cup crumbled goat cheese
- Salt and pepper, to taste
- Fresh herbs, such as parsley or chives, for garnish

Directions:

1. Preheat your oven to 350°F (175°C).
2. In a large bowl, whisk together the eggs and milk or cream until well combined. Season with salt and pepper.
3. Heat the olive oil in an oven-safe skillet over medium heat. Add the diced onion and bell pepper, and cook for 3-4 minutes until softened.
4. Add the sliced mushrooms to the skillet and cook for another 2-3 minutes until they begin to brown.
5. Add the fresh spinach leaves to the skillet and cook until wilted, about 1-2 minutes.
6. Pour the egg mixture evenly over the vegetables in the skillet. Allow the eggs to cook undisturbed for a few minutes until the edges begin to set.
7. Sprinkle the crumbled goat cheese evenly over the top of the frittata.
8. Transfer the skillet to the preheated oven and bake for 15-20 minutes, or until the frittata is set in the center and golden brown on top.
9. Remove the frittata from the oven and let it cool slightly before slicing.
10. Garnish with fresh herbs before serving.

Nutritional Values (per serving, approximate):

- Calories: 150-200
- Fat: 10-15g
- Carbohydrates: 5-7g
- Protein: 10-12g

DINNER

Day 8 to 14: Dynamic and Satisfying Dinners

Moroccan Chicken with Couscous

Ingredients:

- 4 boneless, skinless chicken thighs

- 1 tablespoon olive oil
- 2 cloves garlic, minced
- 1 teaspoon ground cumin
- 1 teaspoon ground coriander
- 1/2 teaspoon ground cinnamon
- 1/2 teaspoon paprika
- 1/4 teaspoon ground ginger
- Salt and pepper, to taste
- 1 cup couscous
- 1 1/4 cups chicken broth
- 1/4 cup raisins
- 1/4 cup sliced almonds, toasted
- 2 tablespoons chopped fresh cilantro or parsley, for garnish
- Lemon wedges, for serving

Instructions:

1. In a small bowl, combine the minced garlic, ground cumin, ground coriander, ground cinnamon, paprika, ground ginger, salt, and pepper to create a spice rub for the chicken.
2. Rub the spice mixture evenly over the chicken thighs, ensuring they are well coated. Let the chicken marinate for at least 30 minutes to allow the flavors to meld.
3. Heat the olive oil in a large skillet over medium-high heat. Add the marinated chicken thighs to the skillet and cook for 5-6 minutes per side, or until they are golden brown and cooked through.
4. While the chicken is cooking, prepare the couscous. In a medium saucepan, bring the chicken broth to a boil. Stir in the couscous and raisins, then remove the saucepan from the heat and cover. Let the couscous steam for 5 minutes, then fluff it with a fork.
5. Serve the Moroccan chicken alongside the fluffy couscous. Garnish with toasted almonds and chopped fresh cilantro or parsley. Serve with lemon wedges on the side for squeezing over the chicken and couscous.

Nutritional Information:

- Calories: 350-400 per serving
- Fat: 12-15g
- Carbohydrates: 30-35g
- Protein: 25-30g

Zucchini Noodles with Bolognese Sauce

Ingredients:

- 4 medium zucchini
- 1 tablespoon olive oil
- 1 onion, diced
- 2 cloves garlic, minced
- 1 carrot, grated
- 1 celery stalk, diced
- 1 pound lean ground beef or turkey
- 1 can (14 ounces) crushed tomatoes
- 2 tablespoons tomato paste
- 1 teaspoon dried oregano
- 1 teaspoon dried basil
- Salt and pepper, to taste
- Fresh parsley, chopped, for garnish
- Grated Parmesan cheese, for serving (optional)

Instructions:

1. Trim the ends of the zucchini and spiralize them into noodles using a spiralizer. Set aside.
2. Heat olive oil in a large skillet over medium heat. Add the diced onion and cook until translucent, about 3-4 minutes.

3. Add the minced garlic, grated carrot, and diced celery to the skillet. Cook for another 2-3 minutes until the vegetables are softened.
4. Add the ground beef or turkey to the skillet, breaking it up with a spoon, and cook until browned and cooked through.
5. Stir in the crushed tomatoes, tomato paste, dried oregano, and dried basil. Season with salt and pepper to taste. Simmer the sauce for 10-15 minutes to allow the flavors to meld and the sauce to thicken slightly.
6. While the sauce is simmering, heat a separate skillet over medium heat. Add the zucchini noodles and cook for 2-3 minutes until they are just tender but still crisp.
7. Divide the zucchini noodles among serving plates and top with the Bolognese sauce. Garnish with chopped fresh parsley and grated Parmesan cheese, if desired.

Nutritional Information:

- Calories: 250-300 per serving (without Parmesan cheese)
- Fat: 12-15g
- Carbohydrates: 10-15g
- Protein: 20-25g

Grilled Pork Chops with Peach Barbecue Sauce

Ingredients:

- 4 bone-in pork chops
- Salt and pepper, to taste
- 2 peaches, peeled and chopped
- 1/4 cup ketchup
- 2 tablespoons apple cider vinegar
- 2 tablespoons honey
- 1 tablespoon soy sauce
- 1 teaspoon Dijon mustard
- 1 clove garlic, minced
- 1/2 teaspoon smoked paprika
- Olive oil, for brushing

Instructions:

1. Preheat your grill to medium-high heat.
2. Season the pork chops with salt and pepper on both sides.
3. In a blender or food processor, combine the chopped peaches, ketchup, apple cider vinegar, honey, soy sauce, Dijon mustard, minced garlic, and smoked paprika. Blend until smooth.
4. Transfer the peach barbecue sauce to a small saucepan and bring it to a simmer over medium heat. Let it simmer for 8-10 minutes, stirring occasionally, until the sauce has thickened slightly.
5. Brush the grill grates with olive oil to prevent sticking. Place the seasoned pork chops on the grill and cook for 4-5 minutes per side, or until they reach an internal temperature of 145°F (63°C) for medium-rare or 160°F (71°C) for medium.
6. During the last few minutes of grilling, brush the pork chops with the peach barbecue sauce, reserving some sauce for serving.
7. Once the pork chops are cooked through and nicely caramelized, remove them from the grill and let them rest for a few minutes before serving.

8. Serve the grilled pork chops with the remaining peach barbecue sauce on the side.

Nutritional Information:

- Calories: 300-350 per serving
- Fat: 10-15g
- Carbohydrates: 20-25g
- Protein: 25-30g

Vegan Mushroom Stroganoff

Ingredients:

- 8 ounces (225g) fettuccine or pasta of choice
- 2 tablespoons olive oil
- 1 onion, diced
- 3 cloves garlic, minced
- 16 ounces (450g) cremini mushrooms, sliced
- 1 teaspoon dried thyme
- 1 teaspoon dried rosemary
- Salt and pepper, to taste
- 1 tablespoon soy sauce or tamari
- 1 tablespoon all-purpose flour
- 1 cup (240ml) vegetable broth
- 1 cup (240ml) canned coconut milk
- 2 tablespoons nutritional yeast (optional)
- Fresh parsley, chopped, for garnish

Instructions:

1. Cook the fettuccine according to the package instructions until al dente. Drain and set aside.
2. Heat the olive oil in a large skillet over medium heat. Add the diced onion and cook until translucent, about 3-4 minutes.
3. Add the minced garlic to the skillet and cook for another minute until fragrant.
4. Add the sliced mushrooms to the skillet and cook until they release their moisture and become golden brown, about 8-10 minutes.
5. Stir in the dried thyme, dried rosemary, salt, pepper, and soy sauce or tamari. Cook for another 2-3 minutes to allow the flavors to meld.
6. Sprinkle the flour over the mushroom mixture and stir to coat the mushrooms evenly.
7. Slowly pour in the vegetable broth, stirring constantly to prevent lumps from forming. Bring the mixture to a simmer and cook for 2-3 minutes until slightly thickened.
8. Pour in the coconut milk and nutritional yeast, if using, and stir until well combined. Simmer the sauce for another 5 minutes, stirring occasionally, until it has thickened to your desired consistency.
9. Taste and adjust the seasoning, adding more salt and pepper if needed.
10. Serve the vegan mushroom stroganoff over the cooked fettuccine, garnished with chopped fresh parsley.

Nutritional Information:

- Calories: 350-400 per serving
- Fat: 15-20g
- Carbohydrates: 40-45g
- Protein: 10-15g

Seared Tuna with Ginger Soy Glaze and Steamed Greens

Ingredients:

- 2 tuna steaks (6-8 ounces each)

- Salt and pepper, to taste
- 2 tablespoons soy sauce
- 1 tablespoon rice vinegar
- 1 tablespoon honey or maple syrup
- 1 teaspoon grated fresh ginger
- 1 clove garlic, minced
- 1 tablespoon sesame oil
- 2 cups mixed greens (such as spinach, kale, or bok choy)
- Sesame seeds, for garnish
- Sliced green onions, for garnish

Instructions:

1. Season the tuna steaks with salt and pepper on both sides.
2. In a small bowl, whisk together the soy sauce, rice vinegar, honey or maple syrup, grated ginger, and minced garlic to make the ginger soy glaze.
3. Heat the sesame oil in a large skillet over medium-high heat until shimmering.
4. Carefully add the tuna steaks to the skillet and sear for 1-2 minutes on each side, depending on desired doneness. For rare tuna, aim for about 1 minute per side. For medium-rare, sear for about 2 minutes per side. Adjust cooking time based on the thickness of the tuna steaks.
5. Pour the ginger soy glaze over the seared tuna steaks in the skillet, allowing it to coat the fish evenly. Cook for an additional 1-2 minutes, gently spooning the glaze over the tuna, until the glaze thickens slightly and coats the tuna.
6. While the tuna is cooking, steam the mixed greens until tender, about 3-4 minutes.
7. Serve the seared tuna steaks immediately, garnished with sesame seeds and sliced green onions, alongside the steamed greens.

Nutritional Information:

- Calories: 300-350 per serving
- Fat: 10-15g
- Carbohydrates: 10-15g
- Protein: 35-40g

Beef and Broccoli with Brown Rice

Ingredients:

- 1 lb (450g) flank steak, thinly sliced against the grain
- 3 cups broccoli florets
- 2 tablespoons vegetable oil, divided
- 3 cloves garlic, minced
- 1 teaspoon grated fresh ginger
- 1/4 cup low-sodium soy sauce
- 2 tablespoons oyster sauce
- 1 tablespoon brown sugar
- 1 tablespoon cornstarch
- 1/4 cup water
- Cooked brown rice, for serving
- Sesame seeds and sliced green onions, for garnish

Instructions:

1. In a small bowl, whisk together the soy sauce, oyster sauce, brown sugar, cornstarch, and water to make the sauce. Set aside.
2. Heat 1 tablespoon of vegetable oil in a large skillet or wok over high heat.
3. Add the thinly sliced flank steak to the skillet and stir-fry for 2-3

minutes until browned and cooked through. Remove the beef from the skillet and set aside.
4. In the same skillet, add the remaining tablespoon of vegetable oil.
5. Add the minced garlic and grated ginger to the skillet and stir-fry for 30 seconds until fragrant.
6. Add the broccoli florets to the skillet and stir-fry for 2-3 minutes until bright green and tender-crisp.
7. Return the cooked beef to the skillet and pour the sauce over the beef and broccoli.
8. Cook for another 1-2 minutes, stirring constantly, until the sauce thickens and coats the beef and broccoli.
9. Serve the beef and broccoli hot over cooked brown rice, garnished with sesame seeds and sliced green onions.

Nutritional Information:

- Calories: 350-400 per serving (excluding rice)
- Fat: 15-20g
- Carbohydrates: 15-20g
- Protein: 35-40g

Roasted Duck with Orange Sauce and Wild Rice

Ingredients:

- 2 duck breasts
- Salt and pepper, to taste
- 1 cup wild rice
- 2 cups chicken or vegetable broth
- 1 tablespoon olive oil
- 2 cloves garlic, minced
- 1 shallot, finely chopped
- 1/2 cup orange juice
- Zest of 1 orange
- 2 tablespoons honey or maple syrup
- 1 tablespoon soy sauce
- 1 tablespoon balsamic vinegar
- 1 teaspoon cornstarch (optional, for thickening)
- Fresh parsley or green onions, for garnish

Instructions:

1. Preheat your oven to 400°F (200°C).
2. Score the skin of the duck breasts with a sharp knife in a crosshatch pattern. Season both sides of the duck breasts with salt and pepper.
3. In a medium saucepan, combine the wild rice and chicken or vegetable broth. Bring to a boil, then reduce the heat to low, cover, and simmer for 45-50 minutes, or until the rice is tender and the liquid is absorbed.
4. While the rice is cooking, heat a large oven-safe skillet over medium-high heat. Add the duck breasts, skin-side down, and cook for 5-6 minutes until the skin is golden and crispy. Flip the duck breasts over and cook for another 2-3 minutes.
5. Transfer the skillet to the preheated oven and roast the duck breasts for 8-10 minutes for medium-rare, or longer if desired.
6. While the duck is roasting, make the orange sauce. In a small saucepan, heat the olive oil over medium heat. Add the minced garlic and chopped shallot, and sauté until softened and fragrant.

7. Stir in the orange juice, orange zest, honey or maple syrup, soy sauce, and balsamic vinegar. Bring the sauce to a simmer and cook for 5-7 minutes until slightly thickened.
8. If you prefer a thicker sauce, mix the cornstarch with a tablespoon of water to make a slurry. Stir the slurry into the sauce and cook for an additional 1-2 minutes until thickened.
9. Once the duck breasts are cooked to your liking, remove them from the oven and let them rest for a few minutes before slicing.
10. Serve the sliced duck breasts over cooked wild rice, drizzled with the orange sauce. Garnish with fresh parsley or green onions.

Nutritional Information:

- Calories: 400-500 per serving
- Fat: 15-20g
- Carbohydrates: 30-40g
- Protein: 35-40g

SNACKS

Day 8 to 14: Energizing Snack Choices

Edamame with Sea Salt

Ingredients:

- 1 cup edamame (frozen or fresh)
- Sea salt, to taste

Instructions:

1. If using frozen edamame, cook them according to the package instructions. If using fresh edamame, you can steam or boil them until tender, about 5-7 minutes.
2. Once cooked, drain the edamame and transfer them to a serving bowl.
3. Sprinkle the edamame with sea salt to taste.
4. Toss the edamame gently to evenly distribute the sea salt.
5. Serve the edamame as a nutritious and satisfying snack.

Nutritional Information:

- Calories: Approximately 100-120 per serving
- Fat: 3-5g
- Carbohydrates: 8-10g
- Protein: 8-10g

Greek Yogurt with Mixed Berries and Flaxseed

Ingredients:

- 1/2 cup Greek yogurt (plain or flavored)
- 1/4 cup mixed berries (such as strawberries, blueberries, raspberries)
- 1 tablespoon ground flaxseed

Instructions:

1. Spoon the Greek yogurt into a serving bowl or cup.
2. Wash the mixed berries and pat them dry with a paper towel. If using strawberries, hull and slice them.
3. Arrange the mixed berries on top of the Greek yogurt.
4. Sprinkle the ground flaxseed over the berries and yogurt.
5. Serve immediately and enjoy this nutritious and delicious snack!

Nutritional Information:

- Calories: Approximately 150-200 per serving

- Fat: 5-8g
- Carbohydrates: 15-20g
- Protein: 10-15g

Sliced Apple with Almond Butter

Ingredients:

- 1 medium apple (any variety)
- 2 tablespoons almond butter

Instructions:

1. Wash the apple thoroughly and pat it dry with a paper towel.
2. Core the apple and slice it into wedges or rounds, as desired.
3. Place the apple slices on a plate or serving dish.
4. Spoon the almond butter into a small bowl or ramekin for dipping.
5. Dip each apple slice into the almond butter and enjoy!

Nutritional Information:

- Calories: Approximately 200-250 per serving
- Fat: 12-15g
- Carbohydrates: 20-25g
- Protein: 5-7g

Roasted Chickpeas with Chili Powder

Ingredients:

- 1 can (15 ounces) chickpeas (garbanzo beans), drained and rinsed
- 1 tablespoon olive oil
- 1 teaspoon chili powder
- 1/2 teaspoon garlic powder
- 1/2 teaspoon paprika
- Salt, to taste

Instructions:

1. Preheat your oven to 400°F (200°C). Line a baking sheet with parchment paper or foil for easy cleanup.
2. In a bowl, toss the drained and rinsed chickpeas with olive oil until they are evenly coated.
3. Spread the chickpeas in a single layer on the prepared baking sheet.
4. In a small bowl, mix together the chili powder, garlic powder, paprika, and salt.
5. Sprinkle the spice mixture over the chickpeas, tossing them gently to coat.
6. Roast the chickpeas in the preheated oven for 20-30 minutes, shaking the pan occasionally, until they are golden brown and crispy.
7. Remove the chickpeas from the oven and let them cool slightly before serving.

Nutritional Information:

- Calories: Approximately 150-200 per serving
- Fat: 5-8g
- Carbohydrates: 20-25g
- Protein: 5-7g

Mixed Nuts and Dark Chocolate Chips

Ingredients:

- 1/4 cup mixed nuts (such as almonds, walnuts, cashews, and pecans)
- 1 tablespoon dark chocolate chips

Instructions:

1. Measure out the mixed nuts and dark chocolate chips.
2. Combine the mixed nuts and dark chocolate chips in a small bowl.
3. Toss gently to mix them together.
4. Serve and enjoy this delicious and satisfying snack!

Nutritional Information:

- Calories: Approximately 150-200 per serving
- Fat: 10-15g
- Carbohydrates: 10-15g
- Protein: 5-7g

Avocado Slice on Whole Grain Crackers

Ingredients:

- 1 ripe avocado
- Whole grain crackers

Instructions:

1. Cut the avocado in half lengthwise and remove the pit.
2. Scoop out the avocado flesh with a spoon and slice it into thin pieces.
3. Arrange the avocado slices on top of whole grain crackers.
4. Serve and enjoy this simple and nutritious snack!

Nutritional Information:

- Calories: Approximately 150-200 per serving (varies depending on the size of the avocado and number of crackers)
- Fat: 10-15g
- Carbohydrates: 10-15g
- Protein: 2-3g

Cottage Cheese with Sliced Radishes

Ingredients:

- 1 ripe avocado
- Whole grain crackers

Instructions:

1. Cut the avocado in half lengthwise and remove the pit.
2. Scoop out the avocado flesh with a spoon and slice it into thin pieces.
3. Arrange the avocado slices on top of whole grain crackers.
4. Serve and enjoy this simple and nutritious snack!

Nutritional Information:

- Calories: Approximately 150-200 per serving (varies depending on the size of the avocado and number of crackers)
- Fat: 10-15g
- Carbohydrates: 10-15g
- Protein: 2-3g

Savor the creamy texture and rich flavor of avocado paired with the crunch of whole grain crackers for a satisfying and wholesome snack option!

Cottage Cheese with Sliced Radishes

Ingredients:

- 1/2 cup cottage cheese
- 3-4 radishes, thinly sliced
- Optional: black pepper, fresh herbs (such as chives or parsley) for garnish

Instructions:

1. Spoon the cottage cheese into a serving bowl or plate.
2. Wash the radishes thoroughly, trim off the ends, and slice them thinly.
3. Arrange the sliced radishes on top of the cottage cheese.
4. Garnish with a sprinkle of black pepper and fresh herbs, if desired.
5. Serve and enjoy this refreshing and nutritious snack!

Nutritional Information:

- Calories: Approximately 100-150 per serving (varies depending on the amount of cottage cheese and radishes)
- Fat: 3-5g
- Carbohydrates: 5-8g
- Protein: 10-15g

WEEK 3

DEEPENING NUTRITIONAL COMPLEXITY

BREAKFAST
Day 15 to 21: Complex Carbs and Proteins

Buckwheat Pancakes with Raspberry Sauce

Ingredients:

- 1 cup buckwheat flour
- 1 tablespoon baking powder
- 1/4 teaspoon salt
- 1 tablespoon maple syrup or honey
- 1 cup almond milk (or any milk of your choice)
- 1 tablespoon coconut oil, melted
- 1 teaspoon vanilla extract
- Cooking spray or additional coconut oil for greasing the pan

Raspberry Sauce:

- 1 cup fresh or frozen raspberries
- 1 tablespoon maple syrup or honey
- 1 tablespoon water
- Optional: lemon zest for added flavor

Instructions:

1. **Prepare the Raspberry Sauce:**
    - In a small saucepan, combine the raspberries, maple syrup or honey, and water.
    - Cook over medium heat, stirring occasionally, until the raspberries break down and the mixture thickens slightly, about 5-7 minutes.
    - Remove from heat and stir in the optional lemon zest. Set aside to cool.
2. **Prepare the Pancake Batter:**
    - In a large mixing bowl, whisk together the buckwheat flour, baking powder, and salt.
    - In a separate bowl, whisk together the maple syrup or honey, almond milk, melted coconut oil, and vanilla extract.
    - Pour the wet ingredients into the dry ingredients and stir until just combined. Do not overmix; a few lumps are okay.
3. **Cook the Pancakes:**
    - Heat a non-stick skillet or griddle over medium heat and lightly grease with cooking spray or coconut oil.
    - Pour about 1/4 cup of batter onto the skillet for each pancake.
    - Cook until bubbles form on the surface of the pancake and the edges look set, about 2-3 minutes.
    - Flip the pancakes and cook for an additional 1-2 minutes, or until golden brown and cooked through.
    - Repeat with the remaining batter, greasing the skillet as needed.
4. **Serve:**

- Stack the pancakes on a plate and top with the raspberry sauce.
- Optionally, garnish with additional fresh raspberries or a drizzle of maple syrup.
- Serve warm and enjoy!

Nutritional Information (per serving, without additional toppings):

- Calories: Approximately 200-250
- Fat: 5-8g
- Carbohydrates: 35-40g
- Protein: 5-7g

Savory Oatmeal with Cheddar and Scallions

Ingredients:

- 1/2 cup rolled oats
- 1 cup water or vegetable broth
- Salt, to taste
- 1/4 cup shredded cheddar cheese
- 1-2 tablespoons chopped scallions (green onions)
- Optional toppings: fried or poached egg, avocado slices, hot sauce

Instructions:

1. **Cook the Oatmeal:**
    - In a small saucepan, bring the water or vegetable broth to a boil.
    - Stir in the rolled oats and a pinch of salt. Reduce the heat to low and simmer, uncovered, for 5-7 minutes, stirring occasionally, until the oats are creamy and tender.
2. **Add Cheese and Scallions:**
    - Once the oatmeal reaches your desired consistency, stir in the shredded cheddar cheese until melted and creamy.
    - Add the chopped scallions and stir to combine.
3. **Serve:**
    - Transfer the savory oatmeal to a bowl.
    - Garnish with additional shredded cheddar cheese and scallions, if desired.
    - Optionally, top with a fried or poached egg, avocado slices, or a drizzle of hot sauce for extra flavor.
    - Serve hot and enjoy this comforting and satisfying breakfast!

Nutritional Information (per serving, without additional toppings):

- Calories: Approximately 200-250
- Fat: 7-10g
- Carbohydrates: 25-30g
- Protein: 8-10g

Overnight Oats with Chia, Pumpkin Seeds, and Pomegranate

Ingredients:

- 1/2 cup rolled oats
- 1 tablespoon chia seeds
- 1 tablespoon pumpkin seeds
- 1/2 cup unsweetened almond milk (or any milk of your choice)
- 1/4 cup Greek yogurt
- 1 tablespoon maple syrup or honey (optional, for sweetness)
- 1/4 cup pomegranate arils (seeds)
- Optional toppings: additional pumpkin seeds, sliced almonds, fresh fruit

Instructions:

1. **Combine Ingredients:**
    - In a Mason jar or airtight container, add the rolled oats, chia seeds, pumpkin seeds, almond milk, Greek yogurt, and maple syrup or honey (if using).
    - Stir or shake well to combine all the ingredients.
2. **Refrigerate Overnight:**
    - Cover the jar or container and refrigerate overnight, or for at least 4 hours, to allow the oats and chia seeds to absorb the liquid and soften.
3. **Add Pomegranate Seeds:**
    - Before serving, stir in the pomegranate arils (seeds) to add a burst of freshness and flavor to the oats.
4. **Serve:**
    - Give the overnight oats a final stir.
    - Optionally, garnish with additional pumpkin seeds, sliced almonds, or fresh fruit for extra texture and sweetness.
    - Enjoy these creamy and nutritious overnight oats straight from the fridge for a convenient and satisfying breakfast!

Nutritional Information (per serving, without optional toppings):

- Calories: Approximately 250-300
- Fat: 10-12g
- Carbohydrates: 30-35g
- Protein: 10-12g

Protein Shake with Peanut Butter and Oat Milk

Ingredients:

- 1 scoop of your favorite protein powder (vanilla or chocolate flavor works well)
- 1 tablespoon natural peanut butter (creamy or chunky)
- 1 cup oat milk (or any milk of your choice)
- 1 ripe banana, frozen (optional, for creaminess)
- 1 tablespoon honey or maple syrup (optional, for sweetness)
- Handful of ice cubes

Instructions:

1. **Combine Ingredients:**
    - In a blender, add the protein powder, natural peanut butter, oat milk, frozen banana (if using), honey or maple syrup (if using), and ice cubes.
2. **Blend Until Smooth:**
    - Blend on high speed until all the ingredients are well combined and the shake is smooth and creamy. If the shake is too thick, you can add more oat milk to reach your desired consistency.
3. **Serve:**
    - Pour the protein shake into a glass.
    - Optionally, garnish with a sprinkle of crushed peanuts or a drizzle of peanut butter on top.
    - Enjoy immediately as a nutritious and satisfying

breakfast or post-workout refuel!

Nutritional Information (per serving):

- Calories: Approximately 350-400
- Fat: 15-20g
- Carbohydrates: 30-40g
- Protein: 20-25g

Whole Grain Waffles with Strawberry Compote

Ingredients:

- 1 cup whole wheat flour
- 1/2 cup rolled oats
- 2 teaspoons baking powder
- 1/4 teaspoon salt
- 1 tablespoon honey or maple syrup
- 1 cup unsweetened almond milk (or any milk of your choice)
- 2 tablespoons unsalted butter, melted (or coconut oil)
- 1 large egg
- 1 teaspoon vanilla extract

For the Strawberry Compote:

- 2 cups fresh strawberries, hulled and sliced
- 2 tablespoons honey or maple syrup
- 1 tablespoon lemon juice
- 1/2 teaspoon vanilla extract

Instructions:

1. Prepare the Waffle Batter:

- In a large mixing bowl, whisk together the whole wheat flour, rolled oats, baking powder, and salt.
- In another bowl, whisk together the honey or maple syrup, almond milk, melted butter or coconut oil, egg, and vanilla extract.
- Pour the wet ingredients into the dry ingredients and stir until just combined. Be careful not to overmix; a few lumps in the batter are okay.
- Let the batter rest for about 5 minutes while you preheat your waffle iron.

2. Preheat the Waffle Iron:

- Preheat your waffle iron according to the manufacturer's instructions.

3. Cook the Waffles:

- Once the waffle iron is heated, lightly grease it with cooking spray or brush with melted butter.
- Pour enough batter onto the waffle iron to cover the waffle grid, using a ladle or measuring cup. Close the lid and cook according to the manufacturer's instructions, until the waffles are golden brown and crisp.
- Repeat with the remaining batter, spraying or brushing the waffle iron with more oil as needed.

4. Make the Strawberry Compote:

- In a small saucepan, combine the sliced strawberries, honey or maple syrup, lemon juice, and vanilla extract.
- Cook over medium heat, stirring occasionally, until the strawberries soften and release their juices, and the mixture thickens slightly, about 5-7 minutes.
- Remove from heat and let cool slightly.

5. Serve:

- Serve the whole grain waffles warm, topped with the strawberry compote.

- Optionally, garnish with additional sliced strawberries and a drizzle of honey or maple syrup.
- Enjoy these wholesome and delicious waffles with a burst of sweet and tangy strawberry flavor for a delightful breakfast or brunch!

Nutritional Information (per serving, waffles only):

- Calories: Approximately 200-250
- Fat: 7-10g
- Carbohydrates: 30-35g
- Protein: 5-7g

Eggs Benedict with Spinach and Avocado

Ingredients:

- 4 large eggs
- 2 English muffins, split and toasted
- 2 cups fresh spinach leaves
- 1 ripe avocado, sliced
- 4 slices Canadian bacon or smoked salmon (optional)
- Hollandaise sauce (homemade or store-bought)
- Salt and pepper, to taste
- Fresh chives or parsley, for garnish (optional)

For Hollandaise Sauce:

- 3 large egg yolks
- 1 tablespoon lemon juice
- 1/2 cup unsalted butter, melted
- Pinch of cayenne pepper (optional)
- Salt, to taste

Instructions:

1. Prepare the Hollandaise Sauce:

- In a heatproof bowl, whisk together the egg yolks and lemon juice until well combined.
- Place the bowl over a pot of barely simmering water (double boiler method). Whisk continuously until the mixture thickens slightly, about 2-3 minutes.
- Slowly drizzle in the melted butter while whisking constantly, until the sauce is smooth and thickened. Be sure to incorporate all the butter gradually to avoid curdling.
- Season with a pinch of cayenne pepper and salt to taste. Remove from heat and keep warm while you prepare the rest of the dish. If the sauce becomes too thick, you can whisk in a little warm water to reach your desired consistency.

2. Poach the Eggs:

- Fill a large saucepan with about 2-3 inches of water and bring it to a gentle simmer over medium heat.
- Crack each egg into a small bowl or ramekin.
- Create a gentle whirlpool in the simmering water with a spoon and carefully slide the eggs, one at a time, into the center of the whirlpool.
- Poach the eggs for 3-4 minutes, or until the whites are set but the yolks are still runny. Use a slotted spoon to remove the poached eggs from the water and transfer them to a plate lined with paper towels to drain excess water.

3. Assemble the Eggs Benedict:

- Place a handful of fresh spinach leaves on each toasted English muffin half.

- If using, place a slice of Canadian bacon or smoked salmon on top of the spinach.
- Carefully place a poached egg on each muffin half.
- Arrange sliced avocado over the poached eggs.
- Spoon hollandaise sauce generously over each egg.
- Season with salt and pepper to taste.
- Garnish with fresh chives or parsley, if desired.

4. Serve:

- Serve the eggs Benedict immediately while still warm, accompanied by a side of fresh fruit or roasted potatoes, if desired.
- Enjoy the creamy, indulgent flavors of this classic brunch dish with a nutritious twist, featuring nutrient-rich spinach and creamy avocado!

Yogurt Bowl with Granola and Kiwi

Ingredients:

- 1 cup Greek yogurt (plain or flavored)
- 1/4 cup granola
- 1 ripe kiwi, peeled and sliced
- 1 tablespoon honey or maple syrup (optional)
- Fresh berries, sliced bananas, or other fruits (optional)
- Chia seeds or flaxseeds (optional)
- Nuts or seeds (such as almonds, walnuts, or pumpkin seeds) for added crunch (optional)

Instructions:

1. Prepare the Yogurt:

- Spoon the Greek yogurt into a serving bowl. You can use plain yogurt for a tangy flavor or flavored yogurt for added sweetness.

2. Add the Toppings:

- Sprinkle the granola evenly over the yogurt. You can use your favorite store-bought granola or make homemade granola for a personalized touch.
- Arrange the sliced kiwi on top of the granola. Kiwi adds a refreshing tartness and vibrant color to the yogurt bowl.
- If desired, drizzle honey or maple syrup over the yogurt and toppings for added sweetness.

3. Customize Your Bowl:

- Get creative with additional toppings! Add fresh berries, sliced bananas, or other fruits of your choice to enhance the flavor and nutrition of your yogurt bowl.
- For extra nutritional benefits, sprinkle chia seeds or flaxseeds over the yogurt. These seeds are rich in omega-3 fatty acids, fiber, and antioxidants.
- Incorporate nuts or seeds for added crunch and protein. Almonds, walnuts, or pumpkin seeds are excellent options for a satisfying texture.

4. Serve and Enjoy:

- Serve the yogurt bowl immediately and enjoy it as a nutritious breakfast, snack, or even a light dessert.

- Mix the ingredients together before eating to combine all the flavors and textures.
- Feel free to experiment with different combinations of fruits, nuts, seeds, and sweeteners to create your perfect yogurt bowl!

LUNCH
Day 15 to 21: Rich and Varied Lunches

Lentil Salad with Roasted Beets and Feta

Ingredients:

For the Salad:

- 2 cans of sardines in olive oil, drained
- 4 cups mixed salad greens (such as baby spinach, arugula, and kale)
- 1/2 cup cherry tomatoes, halved
- 1/4 cup sliced red onion
- 1/4 cup sliced cucumber
- 1/4 cup sliced bell pepper (any color)
- 1/4 cup crumbled feta cheese
- 2 tablespoons chopped fresh parsley (optional)
- Lemon wedges, for serving

For the Vinaigrette:

- 3 tablespoons extra virgin olive oil
- 1 tablespoon red wine vinegar
- 1 teaspoon Dijon mustard
- 1 teaspoon honey or maple syrup
- Salt and pepper to taste

Directions:

1. In a small bowl, whisk together the ingredients for the vinaigrette: extra virgin olive oil, red wine vinegar, Dijon mustard, honey or maple syrup, salt, and pepper. Set aside.
2. In a large salad bowl, combine the mixed salad greens, cherry tomatoes, sliced red onion, sliced cucumber, and sliced bell pepper.
3. Add the drained sardines to the salad bowl, breaking them into smaller pieces with a fork if desired.
4. Drizzle the prepared vinaigrette over the salad ingredients and gently toss to coat everything evenly.
5. Sprinkle the crumbled feta cheese and chopped fresh parsley (if using) over the top of the salad.
6. Serve the sardine salad immediately, with lemon wedges on the side for squeezing over the salad.

Nutritional Values (per serving):

- Calories: 280
- Fat: 18g
- Carbohydrates: 8g
- Protein: 20g

Chicken Gyro with Tzatziki Sauce

Ingredients:

For the Chicken Gyro:

- 1 lb (450g) boneless, skinless chicken breasts, thinly sliced
- 2 tablespoons olive oil
- 2 cloves garlic, minced
- 1 teaspoon dried oregano
- 1 teaspoon paprika
- 1/2 teaspoon cumin
- Salt and pepper to taste
- Pita bread or flatbread, for serving
- Sliced tomatoes, onions, and lettuce, for garnish

For the Tzatziki Sauce:

- 1 cup Greek yogurt
- 1/2 cucumber, grated and squeezed to remove excess moisture
- 2 cloves garlic, minced
- 1 tablespoon lemon juice
- 1 tablespoon extra virgin olive oil
- 1 tablespoon chopped fresh dill (or 1 teaspoon dried dill)
- Salt and pepper to taste

Directions:

1. In a bowl, combine the olive oil, minced garlic, dried oregano, paprika, cumin, salt, and pepper. Add the sliced chicken breasts and toss to coat evenly. Let marinate for at least 30 minutes in the refrigerator.
2. While the chicken is marinating, prepare the tzatziki sauce. In another bowl, mix together the Greek yogurt, grated cucumber, minced garlic, lemon juice, extra virgin olive oil, chopped dill, salt, and pepper. Stir until well combined. Refrigerate until ready to use.
3. Preheat a grill or grill pan over medium-high heat. Once hot, add the marinated chicken slices and cook for 4-5 minutes on each side, or until cooked through and nicely browned.
4. Warm the pita bread or flatbread on the grill for a few seconds on each side.
5. To assemble the gyros, place a generous amount of cooked chicken slices on each warmed pita bread. Top with sliced tomatoes, onions, and lettuce. Drizzle with the prepared tzatziki sauce.
6. Serve the chicken gyros immediately, with extra tzatziki sauce on the side for dipping, if desired.

Nutritional Values (per serving, without pita bread and garnishes):

- Calories: 280
- Fat: 14g
- Carbohydrates: 6g
- Protein: 32g

Quinoa Stuffed Peppers

Ingredients:

- 4 large bell peppers (any color)
- 1 cup quinoa, rinsed
- 2 cups vegetable broth or water
- 1 tablespoon olive oil
- 1 small onion, diced
- 2 cloves garlic, minced
- 1 can (15 ounces) black beans, drained and rinsed
- 1 can (14.5 ounces) diced tomatoes, drained
- 1 cup corn kernels (fresh, frozen, or canned)
- 1 teaspoon ground cumin
- 1 teaspoon chili powder
- Salt and pepper to taste
- 1 cup shredded cheese (cheddar, Monterey Jack, or your favorite melting cheese)
- Fresh cilantro or parsley, for garnish (optional)

Directions:

1. Preheat your oven to 375°F (190°C). Grease a baking dish large enough to hold the bell peppers upright.

2. Slice the tops off the bell peppers and remove the seeds and membranes. Place the peppers upright in the prepared baking dish.
3. In a medium saucepan, combine the quinoa and vegetable broth or water. Bring to a boil, then reduce the heat to low, cover, and simmer for about 15 minutes, or until the quinoa is cooked and the liquid is absorbed.
4. In a large skillet, heat the olive oil over medium heat. Add the diced onion and cook until softened, about 5 minutes. Add the minced garlic and cook for another minute, until fragrant.
5. Stir in the black beans, diced tomatoes, corn kernels, ground cumin, chili powder, salt, and pepper. Cook for 5 minutes, allowing the flavors to meld together.
6. Add the cooked quinoa to the skillet with the bean and vegetable mixture. Stir well to combine.
7. Spoon the quinoa mixture into the prepared bell peppers, dividing it evenly among them. Press down gently to pack the filling into each pepper.
8. Sprinkle the shredded cheese over the tops of the stuffed peppers.
9. Cover the baking dish with foil and bake in the preheated oven for 25-30 minutes, or until the peppers are tender and the cheese is melted and bubbly.
10. Remove the foil and bake for an additional 5-10 minutes, or until the cheese is golden brown.
11. Remove the stuffed peppers from the oven and let them cool for a few minutes before serving.
12. Garnish with fresh cilantro or parsley, if desired, before serving.

Nutritional Values (per stuffed pepper):

- Calories: 320
- Fat: 9g
- Carbohydrates: 49g
- Protein: 14g

Grilled Halibut with Tomato Caper Sauce

Ingredients:

- 4 halibut fillets (about 6 ounces each)
- Salt and pepper to taste
- 2 tablespoons olive oil
- 2 cloves garlic, minced
- 1 small onion, finely chopped
- 1 can (14.5 ounces) diced tomatoes
- 2 tablespoons capers, drained
- 1 tablespoon lemon juice
- 1/4 cup fresh parsley, chopped

Directions:

1. Preheat your grill to medium-high heat.
2. Season the halibut fillets with salt and pepper on both sides.
3. Drizzle the halibut fillets with olive oil and rub to coat evenly.
4. Place the halibut fillets on the preheated grill and cook for 4-5 minutes per side, or until the fish is opaque and flakes easily with a fork. Cooking time may vary

depending on the thickness of the fillets.
5. While the halibut is grilling, prepare the tomato caper sauce. In a saucepan, heat 1 tablespoon of olive oil over medium heat. Add the minced garlic and chopped onion, and cook until softened, about 3-4 minutes.
6. Stir in the diced tomatoes and capers. Bring the mixture to a simmer and cook for 5-7 minutes, allowing the flavors to meld together and the sauce to thicken slightly.
7. Remove the saucepan from the heat and stir in the lemon juice and chopped parsley.
8. Once the halibut fillets are cooked through, transfer them to serving plates.
9. Spoon the tomato caper sauce over the grilled halibut fillets.
10. Garnish with additional chopped parsley, if desired, and serve immediately.

Nutritional Values (per serving):

- Calories: 280
- Fat: 12g
- Carbohydrates: 7g
- Protein: 36g

Vegan Lentil and Mushroom Burgers

Ingredients:

- 1 cup cooked lentils
- 2 cups mushrooms, finely chopped
- 1 onion, finely chopped
- 2 cloves garlic, minced
- 1 tablespoon olive oil
- 1 tablespoon soy sauce
- 1 tablespoon tomato paste
- 1 teaspoon ground cumin
- 1 teaspoon paprika
- Salt and pepper to taste
- 1 cup breadcrumbs
- Burger buns
- Lettuce, tomato, onion, and other desired toppings

Directions:

1. In a large skillet, heat the olive oil over medium heat. Add the chopped onion and minced garlic, and sauté until softened, about 3-4 minutes.
2. Add the chopped mushrooms to the skillet and cook until they release their moisture and become tender, about 5-7 minutes.
3. Stir in the cooked lentils, soy sauce, tomato paste, ground cumin, paprika, salt, and pepper. Cook for an additional 2-3 minutes, allowing the flavors to meld together.
4. Transfer the mixture to a large mixing bowl and let it cool slightly.
5. Once cooled, add the breadcrumbs to the lentil and mushroom mixture and stir until well combined. The mixture should hold together when pressed.
6. Divide the mixture into equal portions and shape each portion into a burger patty.
7. Preheat a grill or skillet over medium heat. Lightly oil the grill or skillet to prevent sticking.
8. Cook the lentil and mushroom burgers for 4-5 minutes on each side, or until golden brown and heated through.

9. Serve the burgers on toasted burger buns with your favorite toppings, such as lettuce, tomato, onion, avocado, or vegan mayo.
10. Enjoy your delicious vegan lentil and mushroom burgers!

Nutritional Values (per serving, without bun and toppings):

- Calories: 180
- Fat: 4g
- Carbohydrates: 30g
- Protein: 10g

Roast Beef Wrap with Horseradish Cream and Arugula

Ingredients:

- 8 ounces roast beef, thinly sliced
- 4 large whole wheat or spinach wraps
- 1 cup arugula leaves
- 1/4 cup horseradish cream (store-bought or homemade)
- 1/2 red onion, thinly sliced
- 1 tomato, thinly sliced
- Salt and pepper to taste

Directions:

1. Lay out the wraps on a clean surface.
2. Spread a tablespoon of horseradish cream evenly over each wrap.
3. Divide the roast beef slices among the wraps, arranging them in an even layer on top of the horseradish cream.
4. Top the roast beef with a handful of arugula leaves, spreading them evenly across the surface.
5. Place a few slices of red onion and tomato on top of the arugula.
6. Season with salt and pepper to taste.
7. Starting from one edge, tightly roll up each wrap, folding in the sides as you go to keep the filling secure.
8. Use a sharp knife to slice each wrap in half diagonally, creating two halves.
9. Serve the roast beef wraps immediately, or wrap them tightly in parchment paper or foil for an on-the-go meal.
10. Enjoy your delicious roast beef wraps with horseradish cream and arugula!

Nutritional Values (per wrap):

- Calories: 320
- Fat: 9g
- Carbohydrates: 35g
- Protein: 25g

DINNER

Day 15 to 21: Hearty and Wholesome Dinners

Lemon Garlic Salmon with Asparagus

Ingredients:

- 4 salmon fillets
- 1 bunch of asparagus
- 2 tablespoons olive oil
- 4 cloves garlic, minced
- 1 lemon, sliced
- Salt and pepper to taste
- Fresh parsley for garnish (optional)

Directions:

1. Preheat your oven to 400°F (200°C).
2. Prepare the asparagus by snapping off the tough ends and placing them on a baking sheet.
3. Drizzle the asparagus with 1 tablespoon of olive oil and season

with salt and pepper. Toss to coat evenly.
4. In a small bowl, mix the minced garlic with the remaining olive oil.
5. Place the salmon fillets on the baking sheet with the asparagus. Brush the tops of the salmon with the garlic and olive oil mixture.
6. Lay lemon slices on top of each salmon fillet for added flavor.
7. Bake in the preheated oven for 12-15 minutes, or until the salmon is cooked through and flakes easily with a fork.
8. Garnish with fresh parsley if desired and serve hot.

Nutritional Values (per serving):

- Calories: 320
- Fat: 18g
- Carbohydrates: 5g
- Protein: 34g

Spicy Thai Basil Chicken

Ingredients:

- 1 lb (450g) boneless, skinless chicken breasts, thinly sliced
- 2 tablespoons vegetable oil
- 3 cloves garlic, minced
- 2 red chili peppers, thinly sliced
- 1 onion, thinly sliced
- 1 bell pepper, thinly sliced
- 1 cup fresh basil leaves
- 2 tablespoons soy sauce
- 1 tablespoon fish sauce
- 1 tablespoon oyster sauce
- 1 teaspoon sugar
- Cooked rice, for serving

Directions:

1. Heat the vegetable oil in a large skillet or wok over medium-high heat.
2. Add the minced garlic and sliced chili peppers to the skillet. Stir-fry for about 30 seconds until fragrant.
3. Add the sliced chicken to the skillet and cook until it's no longer pink, about 5-6 minutes.
4. Stir in the sliced onion and bell pepper. Cook for another 2-3 minutes until the vegetables are tender-crisp.
5. In a small bowl, mix together the soy sauce, fish sauce, oyster sauce, and sugar. Pour the sauce over the chicken and vegetables in the skillet.
6. Stir well to combine and cook for an additional 1-2 minutes until everything is heated through.
7. Remove the skillet from heat and stir in the fresh basil leaves until they are wilted.
8. Serve the spicy Thai basil chicken hot over cooked rice.

Nutritional Values (per serving, without rice):

- Calories: 240
- Fat: 12g
- Carbohydrates: 8g
- Protein: 25g

Vegetarian Paella with Saffron Rice

Ingredients:

- 1 cup Arborio rice
- 2 cups vegetable broth
- 1 pinch saffron threads
- 2 tablespoons olive oil
- 1 onion, chopped
- 2 cloves garlic, minced
- 1 red bell pepper, diced
- 1 yellow bell pepper, diced
- 1 zucchini, diced

- 1 cup cherry tomatoes, halved
- 1 cup frozen peas
- 1 teaspoon smoked paprika
- 1/2 teaspoon dried oregano
- Salt and pepper to taste
- Lemon wedges, for serving
- Chopped fresh parsley, for garnish

Directions:

1. In a small bowl, combine the saffron threads with 2 tablespoons of warm water and let it sit for 5-10 minutes to infuse.
2. In a large skillet or paella pan, heat the olive oil over medium heat. Add the chopped onion and minced garlic, and sauté until softened, about 2-3 minutes.
3. Add the diced bell peppers and zucchini to the skillet. Cook for another 5 minutes until the vegetables are slightly tender.
4. Stir in the Arborio rice, smoked paprika, and dried oregano. Cook for 1-2 minutes to toast the rice slightly.
5. Pour the vegetable broth and saffron mixture into the skillet. Bring to a boil, then reduce the heat to low. Cover and simmer for 15-20 minutes, or until the rice is tender and the liquid is absorbed.
6. Once the rice is cooked, stir in the cherry tomatoes and frozen peas. Cover and cook for an additional 5 minutes until the vegetables are heated through.
7. Season the vegetarian paella with salt and pepper to taste. Garnish with chopped fresh parsley and serve hot with lemon wedges on the side.

Nutritional Values (per serving):

- Calories: 280
- Fat: 7g
- Carbohydrates: 50g
- Protein: 6g

Roast Lamb with Mint Pesto

Ingredients:

- 1 leg of lamb (about 4-5 pounds)
- 4 cloves garlic, minced
- 2 tablespoons olive oil
- 1 tablespoon fresh rosemary, chopped
- 1 tablespoon fresh thyme, chopped
- Salt and pepper to taste

Mint Pesto:

- 2 cups fresh mint leaves, packed
- 1/2 cup fresh parsley leaves, packed
- 1/4 cup walnuts or pine nuts
- 2 cloves garlic
- 1/4 cup grated Parmesan cheese
- 1/2 cup olive oil
- Salt and pepper to taste

Directions:

1. Preheat your oven to 350°F (175°C).
2. In a small bowl, combine the minced garlic, olive oil, chopped rosemary, and chopped thyme to make a marinade for the lamb.
3. Rub the marinade all over the leg of lamb, making sure to coat it evenly. Season the lamb generously with salt and pepper.
4. Place the lamb on a roasting rack in a roasting pan, fat side up.
5. Roast the lamb in the preheated oven for about 1 1/2 to 2 hours, or until it reaches your desired level of doneness. For medium-rare, the

internal temperature should register 145°F (63°C) on a meat thermometer.
6. While the lamb is roasting, prepare the mint pesto. In a food processor, combine the fresh mint leaves, parsley leaves, walnuts or pine nuts, garlic, and Parmesan cheese. Pulse until the ingredients are finely chopped.
7. With the food processor running, gradually drizzle in the olive oil until the pesto reaches your desired consistency. Season with salt and pepper to taste.
8. Once the lamb is cooked, remove it from the oven and let it rest for about 10-15 minutes before carving.
9. Serve the roast lamb with the mint pesto on the side, and enjoy!

Nutritional Values (per serving):

- Calories: 450
- Fat: 30g
- Carbohydrates: 1g
- Protein: 40g

Stuffed Turkey Breast with Spinach and Walnuts

Ingredients:

- 1 turkey breast, boneless and skinless (about 2-3 pounds)
- 2 cups fresh spinach leaves
- 1/2 cup walnuts, chopped
- 1/4 cup feta cheese, crumbled
- 2 cloves garlic, minced
- 1 tablespoon olive oil
- Salt and pepper to taste
- Kitchen twine or toothpicks

Directions:

1. Preheat your oven to 375°F (190°C).
2. Place the turkey breast on a cutting board and butterfly it by making a horizontal cut along one side, but not cutting all the way through, then open it like a book.
3. Season the inside of the turkey breast with salt and pepper.
4. In a skillet, heat the olive oil over medium heat. Add the minced garlic and cook until fragrant, about 1 minute.
5. Add the fresh spinach to the skillet and cook until wilted, about 2-3 minutes. Remove from heat and let cool slightly.
6. Once cooled, spread the cooked spinach evenly over the surface of the opened turkey breast.
7. Sprinkle the chopped walnuts and crumbled feta cheese over the spinach layer.
8. Carefully roll up the turkey breast, starting from one end, to enclose the filling. Use kitchen twine or toothpicks to secure the roll.
9. Place the stuffed turkey breast on a greased baking dish, seam side down.
10. Season the outside of the turkey breast with salt and pepper.
11. Roast in the preheated oven for about 1 to 1 1/2 hours, or until the internal temperature reaches 165°F (74°C) when tested with a meat thermometer.
12. Once cooked, remove the stuffed turkey breast from the oven and let it rest for about 10 minutes before slicing.

13. Slice the stuffed turkey breast into thick slices and serve warm.

Nutritional Values (per serving):

- Calories: 280
- Fat: 12g
- Carbohydrates: 3g
- Protein: 38g

Vegan Chili with Sweet Potato

Ingredients:

- 2 tablespoons olive oil
- 1 onion, diced
- 3 cloves garlic, minced
- 1 bell pepper, diced
- 2 medium sweet potatoes, peeled and diced
- 1 can (15 ounces) black beans, drained and rinsed
- 1 can (15 ounces) kidney beans, drained and rinsed
- 1 can (15 ounces) diced tomatoes
- 1 cup vegetable broth
- 2 tablespoons tomato paste
- 2 teaspoons chili powder
- 1 teaspoon ground cumin
- 1 teaspoon smoked paprika
- Salt and pepper to taste
- Fresh cilantro, chopped (for garnish)
- Avocado slices (for garnish)
- Lime wedges (for serving)

Directions:

1. Heat the olive oil in a large pot over medium heat. Add the diced onion and cook until softened, about 5 minutes.
2. Add the minced garlic and diced bell pepper to the pot, and cook for another 2-3 minutes.
3. Stir in the diced sweet potatoes and cook for 5 minutes, allowing them to slightly brown.
4. Add the drained black beans, kidney beans, diced tomatoes, vegetable broth, tomato paste, chili powder, ground cumin, and smoked paprika to the pot. Stir well to combine.
5. Bring the chili to a simmer, then reduce the heat to low. Cover and let it cook for about 20-25 minutes, or until the sweet potatoes are tender.
6. Season the chili with salt and pepper to taste.
7. Serve the vegan chili hot, garnished with chopped fresh cilantro and avocado slices. Squeeze some fresh lime juice over each serving for an extra burst of flavor.

Nutritional Values (per serving):

- Calories: 280
- Fat: 7g
- Carbohydrates: 47g
- Protein: 9g

Seared Scallops with Polenta and Roasted Tomatoes

Ingredients:

For the Scallops:

- 12 large sea scallops, patted dry
- Salt and black pepper to taste
- 2 tablespoons olive oil
- 2 cloves garlic, minced
- 1 tablespoon unsalted butter
- 1 tablespoon chopped fresh parsley (for garnish)
- Lemon wedges (for serving)

For the Polenta:

- 1 cup polenta (cornmeal)
- 4 cups water or vegetable broth
- Salt to taste
- 1/4 cup grated Parmesan cheese

For the Roasted Tomatoes:

- 1 pint cherry tomatoes
- 2 tablespoons olive oil
- Salt and black pepper to taste
- 2 cloves garlic, minced
- 1 tablespoon balsamic vinegar
- 1 tablespoon chopped fresh basil (for garnish)

Directions:

1. **Prepare the Polenta:**
    - In a medium saucepan, bring the water or vegetable broth to a boil. Add salt to taste.
    - Gradually whisk in the polenta, stirring constantly to prevent lumps.
    - Reduce the heat to low and simmer, stirring frequently, until the polenta is thick and creamy, about 20-25 minutes.
    - Stir in the grated Parmesan cheese until melted. Keep warm.
2. **Roast the Tomatoes:**
    - Preheat the oven to 400°F (200°C).
    - Place the cherry tomatoes on a baking sheet. Drizzle with olive oil and season with salt and black pepper. Toss to coat.
    - Roast in the preheated oven for 15-20 minutes, or until the tomatoes are softened and starting to burst.
    - Remove from the oven and toss the roasted tomatoes with minced garlic, balsamic vinegar, and chopped fresh basil. Set aside.
3. **Prepare the Scallops:**
    - Pat the scallops dry with paper towels and season both sides with salt and black pepper.
    - Heat the olive oil in a large skillet over medium-high heat until shimmering.
    - Add the scallops to the skillet, making sure they are not crowded. Cook for 2-3 minutes on each side, or until golden brown and cooked through.
    - During the last minute of cooking, add the minced garlic and butter to the skillet. Spoon the melted butter over the scallops as they cook.
    - Once cooked, remove the scallops from the skillet and set aside.
4. **Assemble the Dish:**
    - Spoon a portion of the creamy polenta onto each plate.
    - Top the polenta with the seared scallops.
    - Arrange the roasted tomatoes around the scallops.
    - Garnish with chopped fresh parsley and serve immediately with lemon wedges on the side.

Nutritional Values (per serving):

- Calories: 380
- Fat: 20g
- Carbohydrates: 28g
- Protein: 22g

SNACKS

Day 15 to 21: Nutrient-Dense Snacks

Fresh Vegetable Spring Rolls with Peanut Dipping Sauce

Ingredients:

- Rice paper wrappers
- Assorted vegetables (such as carrots, cucumber, bell peppers, lettuce, and avocado), julienned or thinly sliced
- Fresh herbs (such as mint, basil, and cilantro)
- Rice noodles, cooked and cooled (optional)
- Peanut butter: 2 tablespoons
- Soy sauce: 2 tablespoons
- Lime juice: 1 tablespoon
- Honey or maple syrup: 1 tablespoon
- Sriracha sauce (optional): 1 teaspoon
- Crushed peanuts (for garnish)
- Sesame seeds (for garnish)

Directions:

1. Prepare the peanut dipping sauce by whisking together peanut butter, soy sauce, lime juice, honey or maple syrup, and sriracha sauce (if using) in a bowl until smooth.
2. Fill a shallow dish or pie plate with warm water. Submerge one rice paper wrapper into the water for 5-10 seconds until it softens.
3. Remove the wrapper and place it flat on a clean surface.
4. Arrange a small portion of rice noodles (if using), assorted vegetables, and fresh herbs in the center of the wrapper.
5. Fold the bottom edge of the wrapper over the filling, then fold in the sides, and roll tightly to seal.
6. Repeat the process with the remaining ingredients.
7. Serve the spring rolls with the prepared peanut dipping sauce.
8. Garnish with crushed peanuts and sesame seeds before serving.

Nutritional Values (per serving, without rice noodles):

- Calories: 80
- Fat: 5g
- Carbohydrates: 7g
- Protein: 3g

Nutritional Values (per serving, with rice noodles):

- Calories: 120
- Fat: 5g
- Carbohydrates: 16g
- Protein: 4g

Spiced Pear Slices with Honey Drizzle

Ingredients:

- Ripe pears: 2
- Ground cinnamon: 1/2 teaspoon
- Ground nutmeg: 1/4 teaspoon
- Honey: 2 tablespoons
- Lemon juice: 1 tablespoon
- Chopped walnuts or pecans (optional): 2 tablespoons

Directions:

1. Wash the pears thoroughly and pat them dry with a paper towel.

2. Cut the pears into thin slices, removing the core and seeds.
3. In a small bowl, mix together the ground cinnamon and ground nutmeg.
4. Arrange the pear slices on a serving plate or platter.
5. Drizzle the lemon juice over the pear slices to prevent browning.
6. Sprinkle the spiced cinnamon and nutmeg mixture evenly over the pear slices.
7. Drizzle the honey over the spiced pear slices.
8. Optionally, sprinkle chopped walnuts or pecans over the top for added crunch and flavor.
9. Serve immediately and enjoy as a delicious and nutritious snack.

Nutritional Values (per serving, without nuts):

- Calories: 100
- Fat: 0g
- Carbohydrates: 27g
- Protein: 1g

Nutritional Values (per serving, with nuts):

- Calories: 150
- Fat: 6g
- Carbohydrates: 27g
- Protein: 2g

Kale Chips with Nutritional Yeast

Ingredients:

- Fresh kale leaves: 1 bunch
- Olive oil: 1 tablespoon
- Nutritional yeast: 2 tablespoons
- Salt: 1/2 teaspoon

Directions:

1. Preheat your oven to 300°F (150°C) and line a baking sheet with parchment paper.
2. Wash the kale leaves thoroughly and dry them completely using a salad spinner or paper towels.
3. Remove the tough stems from the kale leaves and tear them into bite-sized pieces.
4. In a large bowl, drizzle the kale pieces with olive oil and toss them gently to coat evenly.
5. Sprinkle the nutritional yeast and salt over the kale, ensuring all pieces are seasoned.
6. Spread the kale pieces out in a single layer on the prepared baking sheet.
7. Bake in the preheated oven for 10-15 minutes, or until the kale chips are crispy but not burnt.
8. Remove the baking sheet from the oven and let the kale chips cool for a few minutes before serving.
9. Enjoy your crunchy and nutritious kale chips as a guilt-free snack!

Nutritional Values (per serving):

- Calories: 50
- Fat: 2g
- Carbohydrates: 6g
- Protein: 3g

Protein Bars Homemade with Nuts and Seeds

Ingredients:

- Rolled oats: 1 cup
- Protein powder (flavor of your choice): 1/2 cup
- Almond butter: 1/2 cup
- Honey or maple syrup: 1/4 cup
- Chia seeds: 2 tablespoons

- Flaxseeds: 2 tablespoons
- Pumpkin seeds: 1/4 cup
- Almonds, chopped: 1/4 cup
- Dark chocolate chips: 1/4 cup (optional)

Directions:

1. In a large mixing bowl, combine the rolled oats and protein powder.
2. Add the almond butter and honey (or maple syrup) to the bowl, and mix until well combined.
3. Stir in the chia seeds, flaxseeds, pumpkin seeds, chopped almonds, and dark chocolate chips (if using), until evenly distributed throughout the mixture.
4. Line a baking dish or pan with parchment paper, leaving some overhang on the sides for easy removal later.
5. Transfer the mixture to the lined baking dish, and press it down firmly and evenly using a spatula or your hands.
6. Place the baking dish in the refrigerator for at least 1-2 hours, or until the mixture is firm and set.
7. Once set, remove the protein bar mixture from the refrigerator and use the parchment paper to lift it out of the dish.
8. Use a sharp knife to cut the mixture into individual bars or squares of your desired size.
9. Store the homemade protein bars in an airtight container in the refrigerator for up to one week, or freeze for longer-term storage.

Nutritional Values (per serving):

- Calories: 200
- Fat: 10g
- Carbohydrates: 20g
- Protein: 10g

Smoked Salmon on Cucumber Rounds

Ingredients:

- English cucumber: 1
- Smoked salmon slices: 100g
- Cream cheese: 1/4 cup
- Fresh dill, chopped: 1 tablespoon
- Lemon juice: 1 teaspoon
- Black pepper: to taste

Directions:

1. Slice the cucumber into thin rounds, about 1/4 inch thick.
2. In a small bowl, mix the cream cheese, chopped fresh dill, lemon juice, and black pepper until well combined.
3. Spread a thin layer of the cream cheese mixture onto each cucumber round.
4. Top each cucumber round with a slice of smoked salmon, folding or arranging it neatly on top of the cream cheese.
5. Garnish with additional fresh dill or a sprinkle of black pepper, if desired.
6. Arrange the smoked salmon-topped cucumber rounds on a serving platter and serve immediately.

Nutritional Values (per serving, approximately 4 cucumber rounds):

- Calories: 100
- Fat: 6g
- Carbohydrates: 2g
- Protein: 10g

Blueberry and Lemon Yogurt Pops

Ingredients:

- Greek yogurt: 2 cups
- Blueberries: 1 cup
- Lemon zest: 1 tablespoon
- Lemon juice: 2 tablespoons
- Honey or maple syrup (optional): 2 tablespoons

Directions:

1. In a blender or food processor, combine the Greek yogurt, blueberries, lemon zest, lemon juice, and honey or maple syrup (if using). Blend until smooth and well combined.
2. Pour the mixture into popsicle molds, filling each mold almost to the top.
3. Insert popsicle sticks into the molds.
4. Place the popsicle molds in the freezer and freeze for at least 4-6 hours, or until the popsicles are completely frozen.
5. Once frozen, remove the popsicles from the molds by running warm water over the outside of the molds for a few seconds. Gently pull the popsicles out of the molds.
6. Serve immediately or store the popsicles in a freezer bag or container in the freezer until ready to enjoy.

Nutritional Values (per serving, one popsicle):

- Calories: 70
- Fat: 0g
- Carbohydrates: 14g
- Protein: 5g

Spicy Pumpkin Seeds

Ingredients:

- Pumpkin seeds (raw, unsalted): 1 cup
- Olive oil: 1 tablespoon
- Chili powder: 1 teaspoon
- Paprika: 1/2 teaspoon
- Garlic powder: 1/2 teaspoon
- Salt: 1/2 teaspoon

Directions:

1. Preheat your oven to 300°F (150°C) and line a baking sheet with parchment paper or a silicone baking mat.
2. In a bowl, toss the pumpkin seeds with olive oil until they are evenly coated.
3. Add the chili powder, paprika, garlic powder, and salt to the bowl. Mix well, ensuring the seeds are coated with the spices.
4. Spread the seasoned pumpkin seeds in a single layer on the prepared baking sheet.
5. Bake in the preheated oven for 25-30 minutes, stirring occasionally, until the pumpkin seeds are golden brown and crispy.
6. Remove the baking sheet from the oven and let the pumpkin seeds cool completely before serving or storing in an airtight container.

Nutritional Values (per serving, about 2 tablespoons):

- Calories: 90
- Fat: 7g
- Carbohydrates: 3g
- Protein: 5g

WEEK 4

PREPARING FOR CONTINUATION BEYOND THE PLAN

BREAKFAST

Day 22 to 28: Energizing and Sustainable Starts

Barley and Apple Porridge with Cinnamon

Ingredients:

- 1 cup barley
- 2 cups water
- 1 applc, diced
- 1 tablespoon honey
- 1/2 teaspoon ground cinnamon
- 1/4 cup chopped nuts (optional)

Directions:

1. In a saucepan, bring water to a boil. Add barley and reduce heat to low. Simmer covered for about 30 minutes or until barley is tender and water is absorbed.
2. In another saucepan, combine diced apple, honey, and cinnamon. Cook over medium heat until the apple is soft and caramelized, about 5-7 minutes.
3. Once the barley is cooked, stir in the caramelized apple mixture.
4. Serve the porridge warm, topped with chopped nuts if desired.

Nutritional Values (per serving):

- Calories: 250
- Fat: 2g
- Carbohydrates: 54g
- Protein: 6g

Smoothie with Kiwi, Spinach, and Protein Powder

Ingredients:

- 2 ripe kiwis, peeled and sliced
- 1 cup fresh spinach leaves
- 1 scoop protein powder (flavor of your choice)
- 1/2 cup Greek yogurt
- 1/2 cup almond milk (or any milk of your choice)
- 1 tablespoon honey or maple syrup (optional)
- Ice cubes (optional)

Directions:

1. Place thc slicсd kiwis, fresh spinach leaves, protein powder, Greek yogurt, almond milk, and honey or maple syrup (if using) into a blender.
2. Blend on high speed until smooth and creamy. If the smoothie is too thick, add more almond milk until you reach your desired consistency.
3. Taste and adjust sweetness if necessary by adding more honey or maple syrup.
4. If desired, add a few ice cubes and blend again until smooth and frothy.
5. Pour the smoothie into glasses and serve immediately.

Nutritional Values (per serving):

- Calories: 250
- Fat: 3g
- Carbohydrates: 40g
- Protein: 20g

French Toast with Agave Syrup and Pecans

Ingredients:

- 4 slices of whole grain bread
- 2 large eggs
- 1/4 cup almond milk (or any milk of your choice)
- 1 teaspoon vanilla extract
- 1/2 teaspoon ground cinnamon
- 1 tablespoon agave syrup (or maple syrup)
- 1/4 cup chopped pecans
- Cooking spray or butter for greasing

Directions:

1. In a shallow bowl, whisk together the eggs, almond milk, vanilla extract, and ground cinnamon until well combined.
2. Heat a non-stick skillet or griddle over medium heat and lightly grease with cooking spray or butter.
3. Dip each slice of bread into the egg mixture, ensuring both sides are well-coated but not soggy.
4. Place the coated bread slices onto the preheated skillet or griddle and cook for 2-3 minutes on each side, or until golden brown and cooked through.
5. Once cooked, transfer the French toast slices to serving plates.
6. Drizzle agave syrup over the French toast and sprinkle with chopped pecans.
7. Serve warm and enjoy!

Nutritional Values (per serving):

- Calories: 280
- Fat: 12g
- Carbohydrates: 30g
- Protein: 11g

Scrambled Eggs with Smoked Salmon and Dill

Ingredients:

- 4 large eggs
- 2 tablespoons milk or cream
- 50g smoked salmon, thinly sliced
- 1 tablespoon fresh dill, chopped
- Salt and pepper to taste
- 1 tablespoon butter or olive oil

Directions:

1. In a bowl, whisk together the eggs and milk until well combined. Season with salt and pepper according to taste.
2. Heat the butter or olive oil in a non-stick skillet over medium heat.
3. Pour the egg mixture into the skillet and let it sit for a few seconds until it begins to set around the edges.
4. Gently stir the eggs with a spatula, folding them over themselves as they continue to cook.
5. When the eggs are almost set but still slightly runny, add the smoked salmon and dill to the skillet.
6. Continue to cook, stirring gently, until the eggs are fully cooked and the salmon is heated through.
7. Remove the skillet from the heat and transfer the scrambled eggs to serving plates.
8. Garnish with additional dill if desired and serve hot.

Nutritional Values (per serving):

- Calories: 250
- Fat: 18g
- Carbohydrates: 1g
- Protein: 20g

Avocado and Cottage Cheese Salad

Ingredients:

- 1 ripe avocado, diced
- 1/2 cup cottage cheese
- 1/4 cup cherry tomatoes, halved
- 1/4 cup cucumber, diced
- 1/4 cup red onion, thinly sliced
- 2 tablespoons fresh cilantro, chopped
- 1 tablespoon olive oil
- 1 tablespoon lemon juice
- Salt and pepper to taste
- Optional: mixed salad greens

Directions:

1. In a large bowl, combine the diced avocado, cottage cheese, cherry tomatoes, cucumber, red onion, and cilantro.
2. Drizzle olive oil and lemon juice over the salad ingredients.
3. Gently toss the salad until everything is evenly coated with the dressing.
4. Season with salt and pepper to taste.
5. If desired, serve the salad over a bed of mixed salad greens for added texture and freshness.
6. Enjoy immediately as a light and nutritious meal or side dish.

Nutritional Values (per serving, without salad greens):

- Calories: 280
- Fat: 22g
- Carbohydrates: 12g
- Protein: 9g

Multi-grain Toast with Ricotta and Blackberries

Ingredients:

- 2 slices of multi-grain bread
- 1/2 cup ricotta cheese
- 1/2 cup fresh blackberries
- Honey or maple syrup, for drizzling (optional)

Directions:

1. Toast the slices of multi-grain bread until golden brown and crispy.
2. Spread a generous layer of ricotta cheese evenly onto each slice of toast.
3. Top the ricotta with fresh blackberries, arranging them in a single layer.
4. Drizzle honey or maple syrup over the blackberries if desired, for added sweetness.
5. Serve immediately and enjoy as a delicious and nutritious breakfast or snack option.

Nutritional Values (per serving):

- Calories: 250
- Fat: 8g
- Carbohydrates: 35g
- Protein: 11g

Breakfast Burrito with Beans and Salsa

Ingredients:

- 2 large flour tortillas
- 1 cup cooked black beans
- 4 large eggs
- 1/2 cup shredded cheddar cheese
- 1/2 cup salsa
- Salt and pepper to taste
- Fresh cilantro, chopped (optional)
- Avocado slices for garnish (optional)

Directions:

1. Warm the flour tortillas in a skillet or microwave until they are pliable.
2. In a separate skillet, scramble the eggs over medium heat until cooked through. Season with salt and pepper to taste.
3. Heat the black beans in a small saucepan or microwave until warmed.
4. Place half of the scrambled eggs onto each tortilla, followed by half of the warmed black beans.
5. Sprinkle shredded cheddar cheese over the eggs and beans on each tortilla.
6. Spoon salsa over the cheese, distributing it evenly.
7. Optional: Garnish with fresh chopped cilantro and avocado slices for added flavor and texture.
8. Fold the sides of each tortilla inward, then roll tightly to form a burrito.
9. Serve immediately, and enjoy this hearty and flavorful breakfast option.

Nutritional Values (per serving):

- Calories: 420
- Fat: 17g
- Carbohydrates: 43g
- Protein: 23g

LUNCH
Day 22 to 28: Lunches to Power Through the Day

Kale and Quinoa Salad with Avocado Dressing

Ingredients:

- 1 cup quinoa, cooked and cooled
- 2 cups kale, chopped
- 1 avocado, ripe
- 1 tablespoon olive oil
- 1 tablespoon lemon juice
- Salt and pepper to taste
- Optional toppings: cherry tomatoes, cucumber, red onion, roasted chickpeas

Directions:

1. In a large mixing bowl, combine the cooked quinoa and chopped kale.
2. In a blender or food processor, blend the ripe avocado, olive oil, and lemon juice until smooth to make the avocado dressing.
3. Pour the avocado dressing over the quinoa and kale mixture. Toss until the salad is evenly coated.
4. Season with salt and pepper to taste.
5. Add any optional toppings of your choice, such as cherry tomatoes, cucumber, red onion, or roasted chickpeas.
6. Serve immediately or refrigerate for later. Enjoy!

Nutritional Values (per serving):

- Calories: 320
- Fat: 15g
- Carbohydrates: 40g
- Protein: 10g

Spicy Tofu Stir-Fry with Cashews

Ingredients:

- 14 oz (400g) firm tofu, cubed
- 2 tablespoons soy sauce
- 1 tablespoon sesame oil
- 1 tablespoon cornstarch
- 2 tablespoons vegetable oil
- 2 cloves garlic, minced

- 1 teaspoon ginger, grated
- 1 bell pepper, sliced
- 1 cup broccoli florets
- 1/2 cup cashews
- 2 green onions, chopped
- Cooked rice or noodles, for serving
- Sriracha sauce (optional), for serving

Directions:

1. In a bowl, toss the cubed tofu with soy sauce, sesame oil, and cornstarch until evenly coated. Let it marinate for about 15 minutes.
2. Heat vegetable oil in a large skillet or wok over medium-high heat. Add the marinated tofu cubes and cook until golden brown on all sides. Remove from the skillet and set aside.
3. In the same skillet, add minced garlic and grated ginger. Cook for about 1 minute until fragrant.
4. Add sliced bell pepper and broccoli florets to the skillet. Stir-fry for 3-4 minutes until the vegetables are tender-crisp.
5. Return the cooked tofu to the skillet. Add cashews and chopped green onions. Stir everything together.
6. Cook for an additional 2-3 minutes until everything is heated through.
7. Serve the spicy tofu stir-fry over cooked rice or noodles. Drizzle with Sriracha sauce if desired.

Nutritional Values (per serving):

- Calories: 320
- Fat: 20g
- Carbohydrates: 22g
- Protein: 16g

Grilled Chicken Caesar Pita

Ingredients:

- 2 boneless, skinless chicken breasts
- 2 whole wheat pita bread
- 1 tablespoon olive oil
- Salt and pepper to taste
- 1 cup romaine lettuce, chopped
- 1/4 cup grated Parmesan cheese
- 1/4 cup Caesar dressing
- Cherry tomatoes, halved (optional)
- Red onion, thinly sliced (optional)

Directions:

1. Preheat your grill or grill pan over medium-high heat.
2. Rub the chicken breasts with olive oil and season with salt and pepper.
3. Grill the chicken for about 6-8 minutes per side, or until cooked through and no longer pink in the center. Remove from the grill and let it rest for a few minutes before slicing.
4. While the chicken is resting, warm the pita bread on the grill for about 1-2 minutes on each side until slightly toasted.
5. In a large bowl, toss the chopped romaine lettuce with grated Parmesan cheese and Caesar dressing until well coated.
6. To assemble, place a generous amount of the Caesar salad mixture inside each pita bread.
7. Top with sliced grilled chicken.
8. Optionally, add cherry tomatoes and thinly sliced red onion for extra flavor and texture.

9. Serve immediately and enjoy your delicious Grilled Chicken Caesar Pita!

Nutritional Values (per serving):

- Calories: 380
- Fat: 14g
- Carbohydrates: 29g
- Protein: 35g

Beef Stew with Root Vegetables

Ingredients:

- 1 lb beef stew meat, cubed
- 2 tablespoons olive oil
- 3 cloves garlic, minced
- 1 onion, chopped
- 2 carrots, peeled and chopped
- 2 parsnips, peeled and chopped
- 2 potatoes, peeled and chopped
- 4 cups beef broth
- 1 cup red wine (optional)
- 2 bay leaves
- 1 teaspoon dried thyme
- Salt and pepper to taste
- 2 tablespoons all-purpose flour (optional, for thickening)
- Chopped fresh parsley for garnish

Directions:

1. In a large pot or Dutch oven, heat the olive oil over medium heat. Add the beef stew meat and cook until browned on all sides. Remove the meat from the pot and set aside.
2. In the same pot, add the minced garlic and chopped onion. Cook until softened and fragrant, about 2-3 minutes.
3. Add the chopped carrots, parsnips, and potatoes to the pot. Cook for another 5 minutes, stirring occasionally.
4. Return the browned beef stew meat to the pot. Pour in the beef broth and red wine (if using). Add the bay leaves and dried thyme. Season with salt and pepper to taste.
5. Bring the stew to a boil, then reduce the heat to low. Cover and simmer for 1.5 to 2 hours, or until the beef and vegetables are tender.
6. If you prefer a thicker stew, mix 2 tablespoons of all-purpose flour with a bit of water to form a slurry. Stir the slurry into the stew and simmer for an additional 10-15 minutes until thickened.
7. Once the stew is cooked and thickened to your liking, remove the bay leaves. Taste and adjust seasoning if necessary.
8. Serve the beef stew hot, garnished with chopped fresh parsley for a pop of color and flavor.

Nutritional Values (per serving):

- Calories: 350
- Fat: 12g
- Carbohydrates: 28g
- Protein: 28g

Spinach and Goat Cheese Stuffed Portobello Mushrooms

Ingredients:

- 4 large portobello mushrooms
- 2 cups fresh spinach, chopped
- 1/2 cup crumbled goat cheese
- 2 cloves garlic, minced
- 1 tablespoon olive oil
- Salt and pepper to taste
- Fresh chopped parsley for garnish (optional)

Directions:

1. Preheat your oven to 375°F (190°C). Line a baking sheet with parchment paper.
2. Clean the portobello mushrooms by wiping them with a damp paper towel or gently rinsing and drying them. Remove the stems and scoop out the gills with a spoon to create space for the stuffing.
3. In a skillet, heat the olive oil over medium heat. Add the minced garlic and cook for 1-2 minutes until fragrant.
4. Add the chopped spinach to the skillet and cook until wilted, about 2-3 minutes. Season with salt and pepper to taste.
5. Remove the skillet from the heat and stir in the crumbled goat cheese until combined.
6. Stuff each portobello mushroom cap with the spinach and goat cheese mixture, pressing it down gently to fill the cavity.
7. Place the stuffed mushrooms on the prepared baking sheet and bake in the preheated oven for 15-20 minutes, or until the mushrooms are tender and the filling is lightly browned and bubbly.
8. Once cooked, remove the stuffed mushrooms from the oven and let them cool for a few minutes before serving.
9. Garnish with fresh chopped parsley if desired, and serve warm as a delicious appetizer or side dish.

Nutritional Values (per serving, one mushroom):

- Calories: 120
- Fat: 7g
- Carbohydrates: 6g
- Protein: 8g

Grilled Trout with Walnut Parsley Pesto

Ingredients:

- 4 trout fillets, about 6 ounces each
- 1 cup fresh parsley leaves, packed
- 1/2 cup walnuts, toasted
- 2 cloves garlic, minced
- 1/4 cup grated Parmesan cheese
- 1/4 cup olive oil
- Salt and pepper to taste
- Lemon wedges for serving

Directions:

1. Preheat your grill to medium-high heat.
2. Season the trout fillets with salt and pepper on both sides.
3. In a food processor, combine the parsley, toasted walnuts, minced garlic, and grated Parmesan cheese. Pulse until the mixture is finely chopped.
4. With the food processor running, slowly drizzle in the olive oil until the pesto is well combined and has reached your desired consistency. Season with salt and pepper to taste.
5. Place the trout fillets on the preheated grill, skin-side down. Cook for about 4-5 minutes on each side, or until the fish flakes easily with a fork and is cooked through.
6. While the trout is grilling, spread a generous dollop of the walnut parsley pesto over the top of each fillet.

7. Once the trout is cooked, carefully remove it from the grill and transfer it to a serving platter.
8. Serve the grilled trout immediately with lemon wedges on the side for squeezing over the top.
9. Enjoy your delicious grilled trout with walnut parsley pesto!

Nutritional Values (per serving, one trout fillet with pesto):

- Calories: 380
- Fat: 28g
- Carbohydrates: 2g
- Protein: 32g

Vegan Sushi Rolls with Avocado and Mango

Ingredients:

- 2 nori seaweed sheets
- 1 cup sushi rice
- 2 tablespoons rice vinegar
- 1 tablespoon sugar
- 1/2 teaspoon salt
- 1 ripe avocado, thinly sliced
- 1 ripe mango, thinly sliced
- 1/2 cucumber, thinly sliced
- 1/4 red bell pepper, thinly sliced
- Soy sauce, for serving
- Pickled ginger, for serving
- Wasabi, for serving

Directions:

1. Cook the sushi rice according to the package instructions. Once cooked, transfer it to a large bowl.
2. In a small saucepan, combine the rice vinegar, sugar, and salt. Heat over low heat until the sugar and salt have dissolved, stirring occasionally.
3. Pour the vinegar mixture over the cooked rice and gently fold it in until well combined. Allow the rice to cool to room temperature.
4. Place a nori seaweed sheet on a bamboo sushi mat or a clean kitchen towel, shiny side down.
5. Wet your hands with water to prevent the rice from sticking, then spread a thin layer of sushi rice evenly over the nori sheet, leaving about 1 inch of space at the top edge.
6. Arrange slices of avocado, mango, cucumber, and red bell pepper horizontally across the middle of the rice-covered nori sheet.
7. Starting from the bottom edge closest to you, carefully roll the nori sheet, using the bamboo sushi mat or kitchen towel to help you roll it tightly. Continue rolling until you reach the top edge, then seal the roll by moistening the top edge of the nori sheet with water.
8. Using a sharp knife, slice the sushi roll into 6-8 equal-sized pieces.
9. Repeat the process with the remaining nori sheet and ingredients.
10. Serve the vegan sushi rolls with soy sauce, pickled ginger, and wasabi on the side for dipping.

Nutritional Values (per serving, 1 sushi roll):

- Calories: 160
- Fat: 2g
- Carbohydrates: 32g
- Protein: 3g

DINNER
Day 22 to 28: Flavorful and Fulfilling Evening Meals

Maple Glazed Duck Breast with Bok Choy

Ingredients:

- 2 duck breasts
- 2 tablespoons maple syrup
- 1 tablespoon soy sauce
- 1 tablespoon olive oil
- Salt and pepper to taste
- 2 heads of baby bok choy, halved
- 2 cloves garlic, minced
- 1 tablespoon sesame oil
- Sesame seeds for garnish

Directions:

1. Preheat your oven to 400°F (200°C).
2. Score the skin of the duck breasts in a criss-cross pattern, being careful not to cut into the meat.
3. In a small bowl, mix together the maple syrup, soy sauce, olive oil, salt, and pepper.
4. Brush the maple glaze over both sides of the duck breasts.
5. Place the duck breasts skin side down in an oven-safe skillet or frying pan over medium heat. Cook for 5-6 minutes until the skin is golden brown and crispy.
6. Flip the duck breasts over and transfer the skillet to the preheated oven. Cook for an additional 8-10 minutes for medium-rare or longer if desired.
7. While the duck is cooking, heat the sesame oil in a separate pan over medium heat. Add the minced garlic and cook for 1-2 minutes until fragrant.
8. Add the halved baby bok choy to the pan with the garlic, cut side down. Cook for 3-4 minutes until the bok choy is tender but still crisp.
9. Once the duck breasts are cooked to your liking, remove them from the oven and let them rest for a few minutes before slicing.
10. Serve the sliced duck breasts alongside the sautéed bok choy. Drizzle any remaining maple glaze over the duck and sprinkle with sesame seeds for garnish.

Nutritional Values (per serving):

- Calories: 350
- Fat: 22g
- Carbohydrates: 10g
- Protein: 28g

Spaghetti Carbonara with Turkey Bacon

Ingredients:

- 8 ounces spaghetti or pasta of your choice
- 4 slices turkey bacon, chopped
- 2 cloves garlic, minced
- 2 large eggs
- 1/2 cup grated Parmesan cheese, plus extra for serving
- Salt and black pepper to taste
- Chopped fresh parsley for garnish (optional)

Directions:

1. Cook the spaghetti according to the package instructions until al dente. Drain, reserving 1/2 cup of the pasta water.

2. While the spaghetti is cooking, heat a large skillet over medium heat. Add the chopped turkey bacon and cook until crispy, about 5-6 minutes. Remove the bacon from the skillet and set aside.
3. In the same skillet, add the minced garlic and cook for 1-2 minutes until fragrant.
4. In a small bowl, whisk together the eggs and grated Parmesan cheese until well combined.
5. Return the cooked spaghetti to the skillet with the garlic. Remove the skillet from the heat and quickly pour the egg and cheese mixture over the hot pasta, tossing continuously to coat the spaghetti evenly. The residual heat will cook the eggs without scrambling them.
6. If the pasta seems too dry, gradually add some of the reserved pasta water until the desired consistency is reached.
7. Season the spaghetti carbonara with salt and black pepper to taste.
8. Stir in the crispy turkey bacon until evenly distributed throughout the pasta.
9. Serve the spaghetti carbonara immediately, garnished with extra grated Parmesan cheese and chopped fresh parsley if desired.

Nutritional Values (per serving):

- Calories: 380
- Fat: 12g
- Carbohydrates: 45g
- Protein: 23g

Caribbean Jerk Chicken with Mango Salsa

Ingredients:

- 4 boneless, skinless chicken breasts
- 2 tablespoons olive oil
- 2 tablespoons Caribbean jerk seasoning
- Salt and black pepper to taste
- For the Mango Salsa:
    - 1 ripe mango, peeled and diced
    - 1/2 red onion, finely chopped
    - 1/2 red bell pepper, diced
    - 1/4 cup chopped fresh cilantro
    - Juice of 1 lime
    - Salt to taste

Directions:

1. Preheat the grill to medium-high heat.
2. In a small bowl, combine the olive oil, Caribbean jerk seasoning, salt, and black pepper to make a marinade.
3. Place the chicken breasts in a shallow dish and pour the marinade over them, ensuring they are evenly coated. Let them marinate for at least 30 minutes in the refrigerator.
4. While the chicken is marinating, prepare the mango salsa. In a medium bowl, combine the diced mango, red onion, red bell pepper, cilantro, lime juice, and salt. Mix well and set aside.
5. Remove the chicken breasts from the marinade and discard any excess marinade.

6. Grill the chicken breasts for 6-8 minutes per side, or until cooked through and no longer pink in the center. The internal temperature should reach 165°F (75°C).
7. Once cooked, remove the chicken breasts from the grill and let them rest for a few minutes before serving.
8. Serve the grilled Caribbean jerk chicken with the mango salsa on top or on the side.

Nutritional Values (per serving):

- Calories: 280
- Fat: 10g
- Carbohydrates: 12g
- Protein: 34g

Mushroom and Barley Risotto

Ingredients:

- 1 cup pearl barley
- 4 cups vegetable broth
- 2 tablespoons olive oil
- 1 onion, finely chopped
- 2 cloves garlic, minced
- 8 ounces mushrooms (such as cremini or button), sliced
- 1/2 cup dry white wine (optional)
- 1/4 cup grated Parmesan cheese
- Salt and pepper to taste
- Chopped fresh parsley for garnish

Directions:

1. In a saucepan, bring the vegetable broth to a simmer over medium heat. Keep it warm while preparing the risotto.
2. In a large skillet or pot, heat the olive oil over medium heat. Add the chopped onion and cook until softened, about 5 minutes.
3. Add the minced garlic to the skillet and cook for another minute until fragrant.
4. Add the sliced mushrooms to the skillet and cook until they are golden brown and tender, about 5-7 minutes.
5. Stir in the pearl barley and cook for 1-2 minutes to toast it slightly.
6. If using, pour in the white wine and cook, stirring constantly, until it has been absorbed by the barley.
7. Begin adding the warm vegetable broth to the skillet, one ladleful at a time, stirring frequently and allowing each addition to be absorbed before adding more. Continue this process until the barley is tender and creamy, about 30-40 minutes.
8. Once the barley is cooked to your liking, stir in the grated Parmesan cheese until melted and well combined. Season with salt and pepper to taste.
9. Remove the skillet from the heat and let the risotto rest for a few minutes.
10. Serve the mushroom and barley risotto hot, garnished with chopped fresh parsley.

Nutritional Values (per serving):

- Calories: 280
- Fat: 7g
- Carbohydrates: 45g
- Protein: 9g

Grilled Swordfish with Olive Tapenade

Ingredients:

- 4 swordfish steaks, about 6 ounces each

- Salt and black pepper to taste
- 2 tablespoons olive oil
- 1 lemon, sliced for garnish

For the Olive Tapenade:

- 1 cup pitted Kalamata olives
- 2 tablespoons capers, drained
- 2 cloves garlic, minced
- 2 tablespoons fresh parsley, chopped
- 1 tablespoon lemon juice
- 2 tablespoons olive oil
- Salt and black pepper to taste

Directions:

1. **Prepare the Olive Tapenade:**
    - In a food processor, combine the pitted Kalamata olives, capers, minced garlic, chopped parsley, lemon juice, and olive oil.
    - Pulse the mixture until it forms a coarse paste. Season with salt and black pepper to taste. Set aside.
2. **Preheat the Grill:**
    - Preheat your grill to medium-high heat, about 400°F (200°C).
3. **Season the Swordfish:**
    - Pat the swordfish steaks dry with paper towels. Season both sides with salt and black pepper to taste.
4. **Grill the Swordfish:**
    - Brush both sides of the swordfish steaks with olive oil.
    - Place the swordfish steaks on the preheated grill. Grill for about 4-5 minutes on each side, or until the fish is cooked through and has nice grill marks.
5. **Serve:**
    - Transfer the grilled swordfish steaks to a serving platter.
    - Spoon the olive tapenade over the top of each swordfish steak.
    - Garnish with lemon slices and fresh parsley, if desired.
    - Serve immediately and enjoy!

Nutritional Values (per serving):

- Calories: 320
- Fat: 18g
- Carbohydrates: 5g
- Protein: 35g

Lamb Kofta with Tzatziki Sauce

Ingredients:

For the Lamb Kofta:

- 1 lb ground lamb
- 1 small onion, finely chopped
- 2 cloves garlic, minced
- 1 teaspoon ground cumin
- 1 teaspoon ground coriander
- 1 teaspoon paprika
- 1/2 teaspoon ground cinnamon
- 1/4 teaspoon cayenne pepper (optional)
- Salt and black pepper to taste
- 2 tablespoons chopped fresh parsley
- 2 tablespoons chopped fresh mint
- Olive oil, for grilling

For the Tzatziki Sauce:

- 1 cup Greek yogurt
- 1/2 cucumber, grated and squeezed to remove excess moisture
- 1 clove garlic, minced

- 1 tablespoon fresh lemon juice
- 1 tablespoon chopped fresh dill
- Salt and black pepper to taste

Directions:

1. **Prepare the Lamb Kofta Mixture:**
    - In a large bowl, combine the ground lamb, chopped onion, minced garlic, ground cumin, ground coriander, paprika, cinnamon, cayenne pepper (if using), salt, black pepper, chopped parsley, and chopped mint.
    - Use your hands to mix the ingredients until well combined.
2. **Form the Kofta:**
    - Divide the lamb mixture into equal portions and shape each portion into elongated sausage-like shapes, about 1 inch in diameter and 4-5 inches long. Thread each kofta onto skewers.
3. **Preheat the Grill:**
    - Preheat your grill to medium-high heat.
4. **Grill the Lamb Kofta:**
    - Lightly oil the grill grates to prevent sticking.
    - Place the lamb kofta skewers on the preheated grill. Grill for about 4-5 minutes per side, or until cooked through and nicely browned.
5. **Prepare the Tzatziki Sauce:**
    - In a small bowl, combine the Greek yogurt, grated cucumber, minced garlic, lemon juice, chopped dill, salt, and black pepper. Mix until well combined.
6. **Serve:**
    - Remove the lamb kofta skewers from the grill and transfer them to a serving platter.
    - Serve the lamb kofta hot, with the tzatziki sauce on the side for dipping.
    - Garnish with additional chopped mint and parsley, if desired.
    - Enjoy the delicious flavors of lamb kofta with creamy tzatziki sauce!

Nutritional Values (per serving, including tzatziki sauce):

- Calories: 350
- Fat: 24g
- Carbohydrates: 6g
- Protein: 28g

Vegetarian Gumbo with Okra and Sweet Potatoes

Ingredients:

For the Gumbo:

- 2 tablespoons olive oil
- 1 onion, diced
- 2 bell peppers, diced
- 2 celery stalks, diced
- 3 cloves garlic, minced
- 2 cups diced sweet potatoes
- 1 cup sliced okra (fresh or frozen)
- 1 (14 oz) can diced tomatoes
- 4 cups vegetable broth
- 1 teaspoon paprika
- 1/2 teaspoon dried thyme
- 1/2 teaspoon dried oregano

- 1/4 teaspoon cayenne pepper (adjust to taste)
- Salt and black pepper to taste
- 1 bay leaf
- 1 cup cooked kidney beans
- 1 cup cooked white rice (for serving)
- Chopped fresh parsley, for garnish

Directions:

1. **Sauté the Vegetables:**
    - Heat the olive oil in a large pot over medium heat. Add the diced onion, bell peppers, and celery. Sauté for 5-7 minutes, or until the vegetables are softened.
2. **Add the Aromatics:**
    - Stir in the minced garlic and cook for an additional 1-2 minutes, until fragrant.
3. **Add the Sweet Potatoes and Okra:**
    - Add the diced sweet potatoes and sliced okra to the pot. Stir to combine with the other vegetables.
4. **Season the Gumbo:**
    - Pour in the diced tomatoes and vegetable broth. Add the paprika, dried thyme, dried oregano, cayenne pepper, salt, black pepper, and bay leaf. Stir well to combine.
5. **Simmer the Gumbo:**
    - Bring the mixture to a boil, then reduce the heat to low. Cover the pot and let the gumbo simmer for 20-25 minutes, or until the sweet potatoes are tender.
6. **Add the Beans:**
    - Stir in the cooked kidney beans and let them heat through for a few minutes.
7. **Serve:**
    - Once the gumbo is ready, remove the bay leaf. Taste and adjust the seasoning if needed.
    - Serve the vegetarian gumbo hot over cooked white rice.
    - Garnish each serving with chopped fresh parsley for a pop of color and flavor.

Nutritional Values (per serving, gumbo only, without rice):

- Calories: 220
- Fat: 7g
- Carbohydrates: 35g
- Protein: 6g

Snacks

Day 22 to 28: Delicious and Quick Fixes

Fig and Almond Bites

Ingredients:

- 1 cup dried figs, stems removed
- 1/2 cup almonds
- 1 tablespoon honey
- 1/2 teaspoon vanilla extract
- Pinch of salt

Directions:

1. In a food processor, combine the dried figs, almonds, honey, vanilla extract, and a pinch of salt.
2. Pulse the mixture until it forms a sticky dough-like consistency.
3. Roll the mixture into small bite-sized balls using your hands.
4. Place the fig and almond bites on a parchment-lined baking sheet and

chill in the refrigerator for at least 30 minutes to firm up.
5. Once chilled, transfer the bites to an airtight container and store them in the refrigerator until ready to enjoy.

Nutritional Values (per serving, about 2 bites):

- Calories: 120
- Fat: 6g
- Carbohydrates: 16g
- Protein: 3g

Ricotta and Berry Tartlets

Ingredients:

- 1 sheet puff pastry, thawed
- 1 cup ricotta cheese
- 2 tablespoons honey
- 1 teaspoon vanilla extract
- 1 cup mixed berries (such as strawberries, blueberries, raspberries)
- Fresh mint leaves, for garnish (optional)

Directions:

1. Preheat the oven to 400°F (200°C) and line a baking sheet with parchment paper.
2. Cut the puff pastry sheet into smaller squares or circles, depending on your preference, and place them on the prepared baking sheet.
3. In a small bowl, mix together the ricotta cheese, honey, and vanilla extract until smooth.
4. Spoon a dollop of the ricotta mixture onto each puff pastry square or circle, leaving a border around the edges.
5. Top the ricotta mixture with a few berries, pressing them lightly into the cheese.
6. Bake the tartlets in the preheated oven for 15-18 minutes, or until the puff pastry is golden brown and puffed up.
7. Remove the tartlets from the oven and let them cool slightly before serving.
8. Garnish with fresh mint leaves, if desired, and enjoy!

Nutritional Values (per tartlet):

- Calories: 130
- Fat: 7g
- Carbohydrates: 13g
- Protein: 4g

Beetroot and Goat Cheese Crostini

Ingredients:

- 1 French baguette, sliced into rounds
- 2 medium beetroots, cooked and peeled
- 4 oz (about 120g) goat cheese
- 2 tablespoons olive oil
- 1 tablespoon balsamic glaze
- Fresh thyme leaves, for garnish (optional)
- Salt and pepper to taste

Directions:

1. Preheat the oven to 375°F (190°C).
2. Place the baguette slices on a baking sheet and brush them lightly with olive oil. Season with salt and pepper.
3. Bake the baguette slices in the preheated oven for 8-10 minutes, or until they are crisp and lightly golden.

4. Meanwhile, slice the cooked beetroots into thin rounds.
5. Once the baguette slices are done, remove them from the oven and let them cool slightly.
6. Spread a generous amount of goat cheese onto each baguette slice.
7. Top each crostini with a slice of beetroot.
8. Drizzle the crostini with balsamic glaze and garnish with fresh thyme leaves, if desired.
9. Serve immediately as a delicious appetizer or snack.

Nutritional Values (per crostini):

- Calories: 90
- Fat: 4g
- Carbohydrates: 10g
- Protein: 3g

Avocado Chocolate Mousse

Ingredients:

- 2 ripe avocados, peeled and pitted
- 1/4 cup cocoa powder
- 1/4 cup honey or maple syrup
- 1 teaspoon vanilla extract
- Pinch of salt
- Fresh berries, for garnish (optional)

Directions:

1. In a food processor or blender, combine the ripe avocados, cocoa powder, honey or maple syrup, vanilla extract, and a pinch of salt.
2. Blend the ingredients until smooth and creamy, scraping down the sides of the bowl as needed to ensure everything is well combined.
3. Taste the mousse and adjust the sweetness or cocoa powder to your liking, if necessary.
4. Once smooth, transfer the avocado chocolate mousse to serving bowls or glasses.
5. Cover and refrigerate the mousse for at least 30 minutes to allow it to chill and firm up slightly.
6. Before serving, garnish the mousse with fresh berries, if desired.
7. Serve chilled and enjoy this decadent and nutritious dessert!

Nutritional Values (per serving, without garnish):

- Calories: 160
- Fat: 10g
- Carbohydrates: 18g
- Protein: 3g

Spiced Boiled Eggs

Ingredients:

- 6 eggs
- 1 teaspoon salt
- 1 teaspoon ground cumin
- 1/2 teaspoon ground coriander
- 1/4 teaspoon chili powder
- 1/4 teaspoon paprika
- Fresh cilantro, for garnish (optional)

Directions:

1. Place the eggs in a saucepan and cover them with cold water until they're submerged by about an inch.
2. Add the salt to the water, which helps prevent the eggs from cracking while they boil.
3. Bring the water to a boil over medium-high heat.

4. Once boiling, reduce the heat to low and let the eggs simmer for about 8-10 minutes for hard-boiled eggs, or adjust the time to your preferred level of doneness.
5. While the eggs are boiling, prepare an ice water bath in a large bowl.
6. When the eggs are done, use a slotted spoon to transfer them to the ice water bath to cool down quickly and stop the cooking process.
7. Once the eggs are cool enough to handle, carefully peel off the shells.
8. In a small bowl, mix together the ground cumin, ground coriander, chili powder, and paprika.
9. Roll each peeled egg in the spice mixture until evenly coated.
10. Serve the spiced boiled eggs immediately, or refrigerate them until ready to eat.
11. Optionally, garnish with fresh cilantro before serving.

Nutritional Values (per egg, without garnish):

- Calories: 70
- Fat: 5g
- Carbohydrates: 0.5g
- Protein: 6g

Tomato Bruschetta with Basil

Ingredients:

- 4 ripe tomatoes, diced
- 2 cloves garlic, minced
- 2 tablespoons extra-virgin olive oil
- 1 tablespoon balsamic vinegar
- 1/4 cup fresh basil leaves, chopped
- Salt and pepper, to taste
- Baguette or crusty bread, sliced

Directions:

1. In a mixing bowl, combine the diced tomatoes, minced garlic, extra-virgin olive oil, balsamic vinegar, and chopped basil.
2. Season with salt and pepper to taste, and gently toss until all the ingredients are well combined.
3. Cover the bowl and let the tomato mixture marinate at room temperature for about 15-20 minutes to allow the flavors to meld together.
4. While the tomato mixture is marinating, preheat your oven broiler or grill.
5. Arrange the slices of baguette or crusty bread on a baking sheet or grill pan.
6. Toast the bread slices under the broiler or on the grill for about 1-2 minutes on each side, or until they're lightly golden brown and crispy.
7. Remove the toasted bread from the oven or grill, and let them cool slightly.
8. Spoon the marinated tomato mixture generously over each toasted bread slice.
9. Serve the tomato bruschetta immediately, and enjoy!

Nutritional Values (per serving, estimated for 2 slices of bread with topping):

- Calories: 150
- Fat: 7g
- Carbohydrates: 18g
- Protein: 3g

Matcha Energy Balls
Ingredients:

- 1 cup rolled oats
- 1/2 cup almond butter
- 1/4 cup honey or maple syrup
- 2 tablespoons matcha powder
- 1/4 cup shredded coconut (unsweetened)
- 1/4 cup chopped nuts (such as almonds, cashews, or walnuts)
- 1 teaspoon vanilla extract
- Pinch of salt

Directions:

1. In a large mixing bowl, combine the rolled oats, almond butter, honey or maple syrup, matcha powder, shredded coconut, chopped nuts, vanilla extract, and a pinch of salt.

2. Mix all the ingredients together until well combined. If the mixture seems too dry, you can add a little more almond butter or honey to help bind it together.
3. Once the mixture is evenly mixed, use your hands to roll it into small balls, about 1 inch in diameter.
4. Place the matcha energy balls on a baking sheet lined with parchment paper, and place them in the refrigerator to firm up for at least 30 minutes.
5. Once firm, transfer the energy balls to an airtight container and store them in the refrigerator until ready to eat.
6. Enjoy the matcha energy balls as a quick and nutritious snack whenever you need a boost of energy!

Nutritional Values (per serving, estimated for one energy ball):

- Calories: 90
- Fat: 5g
- Carbohydrates: 10g
- Protein: 2g

SCAN THE QR CODE AND IMMEDIATELY ACCESS YOUR 3 SPECIAL BONUSES IN DIGITAL FORMAT!

🔥 **Bonus 1: Dining Out Without Derailing Your Diet**

🔥 **Bonus 2: Recognizing Your Body Type**

🔥 **Bonus 3: Weekly Grocery Planner**

Made in the USA
Middletown, DE
09 September 2024